THE SEEKER'S GUIDE TO THE

Holy Spirit

Other books in the Seeker Series include

Chicago

THE SEEKER'S GUIDE TO THE

Holy Spirit

Filling Your Life
with Seven Gifts of Grace

LOYOLAPRESS.

CHICAGO

BILL DODDS

LOYOLAPRESS.

3441 N. ASHLAND AVENUE
CHICAGO, ILLINOIS 60657
(800) 621-1008
WWW.LOYOLABOOKS.ORG

The Seeker Series from Loyola Press provides trustworthy guides for your journey of faith. It is dedicated to the principle that asking questions is not only all right, but essential.

Scripture quotations are taken from the New Revised Standard Version Bible: Catholic Edition, copyright © 1993 and 1989 by the Division of Christian Education of the National Council of the Churches of Christ in the U.S.A. Used by permission. All rights reserved.

Cover template and interior design by Lisa Backley
Cover and interior design by Judine O'Shea
Cover photo: © Eryk Fitkau/Getty Images

Library of Congress Cataloging-in-Publication Data
Dodds, Bill.
       The seekers guide to the Holy Spirit : filling your life with seven gifts of grace / Bill Dodds.
              p. cm.
Includes bibliographical references and index.
       ISBN 0-8294-1607-2
    1. Holy Spirit. 2. Gifts, Spiritual. 3. Catholic Church—Doctrines.
I. Title.
       BT121.3.D63 2003
       231'.3—dc22

                                                         2003015169

Printed in the United States of America
03 04 05 06 07 08 09 10 Bang 10 9 8 7 6 5 4 3 2 1

In memory of a grade school classmate
filled with the Spirit at a tender age
Melissa Jean McGinty
1952–1966

Contents

CONTENTS

CHAPTER ONE

Has the Spirit Got a Deal for You!

You have received gifts from the Holy Spirit. The Lord and Giver of Life has been filling your life with amazing grace, whether you realize it or not. What he gives to you is unlike what he gives to anyone else. (Or, if you prefer, what *she* gives to you since the Spirit is neither male nor female.) And, at the same time, what he gives to you is exactly what he gives to everyone else. How is that possible? This amazing grace, these amazing graces, are the gift of himself.

The Spirit and his gifts are what this book is about. Each chapter looks first at the Giver and then at a specific gift and its flip side.

None of us have earned these gifts; neither do we deserve them. They're simply handed to each of us by our all-loving God. What the Spirit brings is a glimpse of the kingdom of God, which Jesus said is among us right now. What the Spirit gives is a bit of heaven on earth.

Then, too, what God offers us is more than any human being can imagine. It's more than can be described or defined or explained or understood. What he offers is love. And he not only loves and can be loved, but he *is* love.

That's one reason why trying to describe the Spirit is a bit like trying to describe the wind. We can't say what the wind looks like; we can only say what it feels like and what we see it doing. That doesn't mean we know nothing about the Holy Spirit. We know a lot because God has chosen to reveal a lot to us. But—let's be honest here—knowing a lot about an infinite and all-powerful Being isn't *really* knowing a lot.

Still, the more we learn of the Spirit, by both getting to know about him (through education) and getting to know him (through the Mass, the sacraments, Scripture, prayer, and service to others), the better we can become at recognizing his gifts. The same holds true in other areas of our life. The better we know the artist, the more easily and readily we recognize one of his paintings—or the musician, her song. Even closer to home, we immediately recognize a loved one's voice on the phone or a note in her handwriting.

A difference, when it comes to the Holy Spirit, is that as we become better at spotting his gifts, the more readily we can put those gifts to use. In a very selfish way—but in a "good" selfish way—we can make our lives better by getting to know the Holy Spirit better.

Every day he offers his gifts. Every day we each have the opportunity, the blessing, to pick one up and use it or get even better at using it.

And just as we can get to know a little bit more about the artist by closely examining his painting, or the musician by carefully listening to her song, we can know more about the Spirit by learning about his gifts.

Rather than a vicious circle, it's a lovely circle. It is, truly, a circle of love—the love that flows from the Father to the Son and from the Son to the Father. The love that is a Person called the Holy Spirit.

Your Creator and Sustainer invites you into that circle, but you can tell him, "No thanks." Because we have free will (yet another incredible gift), we can ignore his gifts. We can turn them down. We can let them gather dust. We can do those things despite the fact that what we each truly want, what we each truly long for, is what the Spirit offers. St. Augustine wrote in the fifth century, "You have made us for yourself, and our hearts are restless until they rest in you." It's amazing grace that gives rest. It's amazing grace that helps us examine the hard questions: "Why am I here?" and "What's my life *really* all about?"

We need that help, that grace, because on our own we can come up with a lot of answers that don't satisfy us, that don't work for us, because they aren't true. It's not hard to fall victim to a cockeyed notion or two because we live in a world steeped in sin, and each of us is a sinner.

One definition of sinning could be choosing the opposite of what the Spirit offers, even if we can't name the grace or the fault. We turn our backs on an opportunity for wisdom and rush headlong into foolishness. We pass up an opportunity for fortitude—for courage—and opt for cowardice.

That's one more reason why knowing the gifts can help us in our daily lives. The more we know hot, the faster we feel the cold. The more we eat the sweet, the faster we taste the bitter.

"Why am I here?" "What's my life really all about?" The answers we come up with will always be true if we allow ourselves to be led by the Spirit. Why? Because it's the Spirit that leads us to Jesus, who is the way, the truth, and the life (John 14:6). We come to the Father through him. It's with the Father, Son, and Spirit that our hearts find rest. It's in the kingdom of God that we find our true home.

Just as Jesus abided by the will of his Father, through the Spirit's amazing grace so too can we become better at understanding and following God's plan for us. That doesn't mean we somehow become less of who we are. It means we become more of who we were created to be.

Following God's plan for us also does not mean that we become robots or automatons for Jesus: cookie-cutter Catholics. The gifts of the Spirit aren't "off the rack." We don't have to force ourselves into them because they're too small or have them bag on us because they're too big. Each is custom designed. The Holy Spirit gives each of us what we need. He hands each of us what will truly help, and—a word of warning here—it may not necessarily be what we would like right then and there.

All of this sounds very abstract, but the gifts of the Holy Spirit aren't. They can't be. They're personal. They're Person to person, God to you.

But . . . it must be said that while what the Spirit offers to each of us can *seem* to pinch or feel baggy at first, in some instances, conforming our will to the Father's is like wearing a stiff new pair of shoes that, in the long run, will become our favorites. Other times, what the Spirit brings seems beyond us. It's just too much. But, again through God's grace, we grow into it. Day by day, opportunity by opportunity, we can increase in wisdom, understanding, knowledge, counsel, piety, fortitude, and fear of the Lord.

That list of seven graces can be found in Isaiah 11:2–3. He describes the coming Messiah this way:

> The spirit of the LORD shall rest on him,
>> the spirit of wisdom and understanding,
>> the spirit of counsel and might,
>> the spirit of knowledge and the fear of the LORD.
> His delight shall be in the fear of the LORD.

(The Hebrew text of Isaiah uses "fear of the Lord" twice in its list of virtues. The Catholic Church's traditional list has "piety" in place of the first "fear of the Lord" because that virtue was named in what's called the Septuagint, the Greek translation of the Hebrew Bible.)

Even though the *Catechism of the Catholic Church* says all seven "belong in their fullness to Christ" (section 1831), at first glance some of them may seem worthwhile to us, while others less so. Perhaps few would blame us if we hesitated before requesting heaping helpings of piety and fear of the Lord. Their value seems questionable unless we know what they really mean. That, of course, is also part of what this book is about. We'll look at each gift and what it truly is, despite an old-fashioned name that doesn't quite grab us in our own time.

The truth is that we each need these seven gifts in our own time, in our own lives, homes, and hearts. As St. Paul put it:

> Now concerning spiritual gifts, brothers and sisters, I do not want you to be uninformed. . . .
>
> [T]here are varieties of gifts, but the same Spirit; and there are varieties of services, but the same Lord; and there are varieties of activities, but it is the same God who activates all of them in everyone. To each is given the manifestation of the Spirit for the common good. . . . All these are activated by one and the same Spirit, who allots to each one individually just as the Spirit chooses. (1 Corinthians 12:1, 4–7, 11)

Come, Holy Spirit

Come, Holy Spirit, fill the hearts of your faithful and enkindle in them the fire of your love.

Send forth your Spirit, and they shall be created.

And you shall renew the face of the earth.

Let us pray. O God, you instructed the hearts of the faithful by the light of the Holy Spirit, grant that by that same Spirit we may be truly wise and ever rejoice in your consolation. Through the same Christ, our Lord, Amen.

CHAPTER TWO

The Spirit in the Trinity

The Gift of Wisdom:
Oh, for a Little Common Sense
in a World Filled
with Foolishness

It's easy to have a wrong or misguided notion about the Trinity because it's hard to understand what the Trinity is.

Actually, for us humans, it's impossible to fully understand it. Again, the more we know, the more we know we don't know, the more we realize we simply can't know, and the more we have to acknowledge that our minds are incapable of knowing.

We have a clue or many clues because God gave them to us. He revealed some things about himself. And when we begin to examine those things, we learn more about him. That, of course, is what life is all about, what *we* are all about. We were created to be with him, to journey back to him, and to spend eternity with him.

Most of us have the advantage of being familiar with the term *Trinity,* the idea of three Persons in one God. We can rattle off "Father, Son, and Holy Spirit" and, if pressed to explain that trio, can fall back on St. Patrick's shamrock. "Three leaves, one stem" is handy but hardly satisfying (and, some Patrick biographers say, not historically accurate).

Coming to a fuller (but still incomplete) understanding of the Trinity is important because that teaching is so central to our lives as Christians. It's how most Christians begin their lives in the church, being formally baptized in the name of the Father and of the Son and of the Holy Spirit. It's how Catholics begin and end most prayers, including the Mass.

At the same time, most of us have the *disadvantage* of being familiar with the term *Trinity*. Unclear of what it might really mean, we wonder even less about where it originated. We simply accept it as one of those "church things." We can't imagine what it would be like to hear this teaching for the first time. And even if we could, we can't imagine what it would be like to hear it out of context and then try to figure out what it means.

That was the task faced by the early church. What we, in the twenty-first century, say about the Trinity is what they—in the centuries soon after Christ—wrestled with and sorted out and came to understand as best they could. That's the way it is with a lot of what we believe because of what's known as the development of doctrine.

Based soundly on Scripture and tradition, teachings—truths—have been looked at and prayed about and questioned. How can Jesus be God and human at the same time?

How can the bread and wine *really* be his body and blood? How can there be a hell if God loves us completely? And on and on.

The truth can't change because God doesn't give us bogus information. The church's examining of that truth, living of that truth, has resulted—time and again—in a deeper understanding of divine revelation.

Our understanding of God, and of ourselves, continues to grow. We continue to "get it" piece by piece because the church is guided by the Holy Spirit, the helper sent to us after Jesus returned to the Father.

We know about the Trinity because God told us about it. We didn't make it up. Scripture scholars point out that there are "hints"—traces—of that teaching in the Old Testament. But the chosen people were even more in the dark than we are because the Incarnation, that is, the Word—Jesus—made flesh, had yet to happen. And the Son had yet to return to the Father, so it wasn't the Holy Spirit's turn.

The *Catechism of the Catholic Church (CCC)* points out that many religions call God "Father." In the Jewish tradition, he gets that title as Creator of the world; as the one who made a covenant with and gave the law (the Torah) to Israel, his "firstborn son" (Exodus 4:22); and as the Father of the king of Israel (*CCC*, section 238). Then, too, he's the Father of the poor, of the widows and orphans under his tender care (see 2 Samuel 7:14 and Psalm 68:5).

THE SPIRIT IN THE TRINITY

These sources tell us two things about the Supreme Being: He is the origin of everything and has authority over everything. And he is goodness and love, caring for his children the way a parent does. The *Catechism* notes that a couple of images of God as a mother can be found in Isaiah 66:13 and Psalm 131:2.

"The language of faith thus draws on the human experience of parents, who are in a way the first representatives of God for man" (*CCC*, section 239). We know human parents mess up. (Those of us who are parents know it all too well.) But just as God transcends the human distinction of male or female, he transcends human fatherhood and motherhood even though he is their origin and standard. Our parenthood goes back to him. We are called to strive to live up to the example he sets, but no human being is a father—a parent—the way God the Father is.

Before the Son was born a human, the chosen people spoke of the Father. They prayed to the Father. They understood there was a relationship between themselves and the Father. That's one reason why what Jesus taught was so startling to them. He said God is also the Father in relation to him, the Son. His only Son. And he, Jesus, is the Son in relation to the Father. Eternally Father. Eternally Son.

That "eternally" didn't just mean going on forever but *having gone on forever.* Their existence, their relationship, had no beginning and will have no end.

In fact, Jesus said, "No one knows the Son except the Father, and no one knows the Father except the Son and anyone to whom the Son chooses to reveal him" (Matthew 11:27). By claiming to be God's only Son, Jesus was saying that he, too, was God. For century after century, the chosen people—and they knew they were chosen—had come to understand some things about the Father, starting with the fact that there is only one God.

And for centuries they had longed for and looked for the Messiah, whom God would send to help them. Many, if not most, assumed this Anointed One was going to rally the troops and restore their nation, which was then under the rule of ironfisted Rome. It would have been easy for those first-century Israelites to write off any hope of Jesus being the true Messiah. Yes, he spoke with authority and performed miracles, but he engaged in no purely political action. And then—what was he thinking and just how stupid did he assume the Jews were?—he said he was God's equal, God's intimate. He said *he* was God.

In the eyes of many, it was blasphemy, pure and simple.

So those who stuck with him, the Twelve and the other disciples, were really going out on a limb. They had to have a tremendous amount of faith in him. The miracles could show he was *of* God and had been sent *by* God, but to claim *Sonship?*

"Who am I?" he asked them. Never mind what others say; what do you say? Simon piped up: "You are the Messiah, the Son of the living God" (Matthew 16:16). But how did Simon know that? It could be that even he didn't know how he knew. But Jesus did. "Flesh and blood has not revealed this to you, but my Father in heaven" (Matthew 16:17). And it was at that point that Jesus changed Simon's name to Peter—to "the Rock." And it was on this Rock, this faith-filled human and this divine revelation, that Christ chose to build his church.

Then Peter and the others started to get it, to really get it. And then Jesus told them about his upcoming death and resurrection. As much as he tried to prepare them, most really weren't ready for that. Even the Rock crumbled. John was the only apostle who hung in there, who witnessed the final hours. And later it would be John, the last living apostle, who would start his own Gospel, his own telling of this Good News, with a description of the relationship between the Father and the Son:

"In the beginning was the Word, and the Word was with God, and the Word was God. . . . And the Word became flesh and lived among us" (John 1:1, 14).

That, of course, was written decades later. It was written long after the helper, the Holy Spirit, had come, just as Jesus had promised. Part of preparing the apostles for his imminent death was comforting them with the assurance that they didn't have to be troubled. Despite what would happen to him, and later to them, it was going to be all right. He was going to get a place ready for each of them in his Father's house (John 14:1–3). Jesus was how they would get there because he was—he is—the way, the truth, and the life. And "no one comes to the Father except through me" (John 14:6).

At this point, the apostles had accepted that the Father and the Son are one. But their minds—like ours—just couldn't fully grasp it. That is why one of them, Philip, asked Jesus to show them the Father, and then, then, they would be satisfied. Jesus replied: You see me, right? If you see me, you see him. "I am in the Father and the Father is in me" (John 14:11).

And if that's too much for you, he continued, believe me because of the miracles. But, I have to tell you, if you believe in me you're going to do even more miracles. Bigger miracles. Why? Because I'm going to the Father and I will do whatever you ask in my name so that the Father will be glorified in the Son.

And if you love me, Jesus added, you're going to keep my commandments and I'm going to ask the Father and he will give you an advocate, a helper, who will be with you forever. That Paraclete (Greek for "advocate") is the Spirit of truth.

Jesus told the apostles a little more about this advocate. The world can't receive this Spirit because "it neither sees him nor knows him." They, however, will know him "because he abides with you, and he will be in you" (John 14:17).

Jesus also told them he wasn't going to leave them orphans. (That's an amazing statement to make to a group of adults who must have, Jesus knew, felt that they were being abandoned.) And further, he acknowledged that he had given

THE SPIRIT IN THE TRINITY

them a lot of information in a very short amount of time. He realized they hadn't absorbed or understood it all.

"But the Advocate, the Holy Spirit, whom the Father will send in my name, will teach you everything, and remind you of all that I have said to you. Peace I leave with you; my peace I give to you. . . . Do not let your hearts be troubled, and do not let them be afraid" (John 14:26–27).

His words could be summed up this way: The bad news is that I'm going to be executed. The good news is that I'm going to rise from the dead. The bad news it that then I'll leave to be with the Father. But that's actually good news because after I leave, we will send the Holy Spirit. The really confusing news: God isn't just Father. God isn't just Father and Son. God is Father, Son, and Holy Spirit.

"When the Advocate comes, whom I will send to you from the Father, the Spirit of truth who comes from the Father, he will testify on my behalf. You also are to testify because you have been with me from the beginning" (John 15:26–27).

They had received a divine revelation.

"I still have many things to say to you," Jesus told them,

> but you cannot bear them now. When the Spirit of truth comes, he will guide you into all the truth; for he will not speak on his own, but will speak whatever he hears, and he will declare to you the things that are

THE SPIRIT IN THE TRINITY

to come. He will glorify me, because he will take what is mine and declare it to you. All that the Father has is mine. For this reason I said that he will take what is mine and declare it to you. (John 16:12–15)

"I tell you the truth: it is to your advantage that I go away, for if I do not go away, the Advocate will not come to you; but if I go, I will send him to you" (John 16:7).

We'll look at that coming, Pentecost, in chapter 3.

The Gift of Wisdom: Oh, for a Little Common Sense in a World Filled with Foolishness

Wisdom is the spiritual gift that enables each of us to know the purpose and plan of God. At the core of the six other gifts of the Spirit, it concerns the "you" that is at the core of "you": your true self. It's a way the Creator has chosen to make it possible for you to know more about him and his creation and your role in it.

This doesn't mean only Christians can value, pursue, or find wisdom. A person of any religion or no religion can do that, just as he or she can value, pursue, and find love. No, the advantage Catholics have is the greater opportunity to know the source—the Source—of wisdom (and of love and all the rest). Through the church and its Mass and sacraments, Catholics have access to the Spirit—to God's grace—in particular ways established by God.

The Greek philosophers Plato and Aristotle prized wisdom; so did the Roman orator and philosopher Cicero. They associated it—sometimes calling it prudence—with justice, fortitude, and temperance. Later St. Ambrose (ca. 340–397) called these the cardinal virtues, from the Latin *cardines,* meaning "hinges." He said all the other virtues are related to, or hinge on, them.

As the ancient Greeks pursued wisdom, one of their groups demonstrated how it's not too hard to get off track doing that. The Sophists—the "wise men"—were traveling teachers who came to specialize in eloquence and persuasion. They reasoned that there is no ultimate truth. What may be true for you may not be true for me, so what is right for you may not be right for me. In the same way, what is wrong for you may not be wrong for me.

In modern idiom, it was talk-show morality. If you have a problem with what I think, say, or do, then you're the one with the problem.

The Sophists said that because truth was so flexible, good and evil could not be discovered. Ditto with distinguishing between justice and injustice and, ultimately, right and wrong. These "wise men" were able to teach their students how to easily and convincingly argue any point of view.

Socrates (who taught Plato, who taught Aristotle) tried to sort all this out and to discover some absolutes when it came to right and wrong, justice and injustice, and the rest. Those three—especially Aristotle—went a long way in examining wisdom, but it wasn't far enough. No, it was another tribe of people—to the southeast of Greece—who fared better. That wasn't because they were so much brighter than the Greeks, but because, piece by piece, they were being given the answers.

Even so, they didn't necessarily understand what was being revealed to them, and they didn't always believe it. These were the Hebrews, the ragtag bunch selected by God— by Yahweh—to be his chosen people. He was their teacher, leading them step by step in the ways of true wisdom, just as he had led them out of Egypt and back to the Promised Land. Just as that desert journey was anything but a simple straight shot, their learning more about the Lord and his ways was difficult, too.

As with just about any culture or group in any age, the children of Abraham valued wisdom. Their knowledge was organized into simple teachings and had an obvious quality that anyone with half a brain would want—the information was useful. Since these things were good to know, folks who didn't want that wisdom or didn't use that wisdom were fools.

Some of the Old Testament shows the common wisdom of the time. There are adages that were popular in other cultures, too (and remain popular in our own time). Some of this common wisdom was the equivalent of sayings such as our "Look both ways before crossing the street" or, less concretely, "Pride goes before a fall."

Over time, the chosen people came to realize that wisdom was more than that. It was both a gift from Yahweh and *of* Yahweh. That was why each person needed wisdom not just in everyday matters, but also in his or her relationship with God. The Hebrew law, which spelled out that relationship, offered wisdom.

So to be wise was both to follow the practical advice—the sayings that read like something from *Poor Richard's Almanack*—and to take to heart what the Jewish Scriptures taught. By the time Christ was born, the "practical" had been absorbed by the "religious." The consensus was that wisdom was both a grace from God and the result of experiences and learning.

In the New Testament, Luke says the boy Jesus grew "in wisdom and in years, and in divine and human favor" (Luke 2:52). Because he was fully human, he learned as we learn and aged as we age. He did so even though, being fully divine, he knew all things and was ageless.

Scripture scholars point out that both the Evangelist-apostle John and the great missionary-apostle Paul show the relationship between wisdom as presented in the Old Testament (which is sometimes personified) and Jesus.

It's Paul who notes that what he was preaching—Christ crucified—seemed to turn wisdom on its head. God sent his Son to save us. Okay. And this God-human did that by being executed. What? That was the best plan God could come up with?

No wonder the Greeks in apostolic times laughed at Paul. But Paul—who was no slouch academically—was not out to dazzle the people who had produced so many top-notch thinkers, philosophers, and rhetoricians. Rather, he explains, Christ sent him "to proclaim the gospel, and not with eloquent wisdom, so that the cross of Christ might not be emptied of its power. For the message about the cross is foolishness to those who are perishing, but to us who are being saved it is the power of God" (1 Corinthians 1:17–18).

"For Jews demand signs and Greeks desire wisdom," he continues, "but we proclaim Christ crucified, a stumbling block to Jews and foolishness to Gentiles, but to those who are the called, both Jews and Greeks, Christ the power of God and the wisdom of God. For God's foolishness is wiser than human wisdom, and God's weakness is stronger than human strength" (1 Corinthians 1:22–25).

Then he offers this warning for those who do follow Jesus: "Consider your own call, brothers and sisters: not many of you were wise by human standards, not many were powerful, not many were of noble birth. But God chose what is foolish in the world to shame the wise; God chose what is weak in the world to shame the strong; God chose what is low and despised in the world. . . . Do not deceive yourselves. If you think that you are wise in this age, you should become fools so that you may become wise. For the wisdom of this world is foolishness with God" (1 Corinthians 1:26–28; 3:18–19).

Paul's words—inspired by the Holy Spirit, who is the source of wisdom—form the foundation of what the church teaches about wisdom and about how Christ redeemed the world. They are at the core of understanding the gift as we each receive it, and of understanding how Christ died to redeem each of us.

Even now, we tend to split wisdom into the categories of practical and religious or spiritual. A standard cartoon mixes the two. The pilgrim finally reaches the summit of the mountain and asks the wise man's counsel. The sage advises: "Don't stick a fork in your toaster."

Practical wisdom has always been considered a prize offered for graduating from the school of hard knocks. More than simply learning from tough times or our own mistakes, wisdom is remembering those lessons and applying them when they're needed.

Fortunately, we can avoid making all the foolish mistakes others have made by paying attention to their sound advice. Unfortunately, at times we all manage to come up with our own personal foolishness.

Then, too, it's possible to "graduate" in one subject—toasters and forks, for instance—and still be in kindergarten when it comes to another area, such as getting along with coworkers. Here's an example:

It's not unusual for the neophyte staff member to spout off and do all sorts of foolish things, such as telling veterans a "better" way to get the job done despite the fact that the veterans have been doing the job for twenty or thirty years. The foolish newcomer sees where improvements can be made (or believes improvements can be made) and immediately, and even at times condescendingly, informs the veterans of where the procedures or personnel are sorely lacking. Equally unwise, he just starts doing the job his way, ignoring how the management wants it done.

What makes this even trickier is that the new worker may be right. Entering with a fresh perspective and no little enthusiasm, he may have a method or style that's much better. It might be one that benefits both the workers and the company's bottom line. But that insight, that grain of wisdom, is lost in the blundering and blustery way he presents it. Good idea, bad presentation, and very bad timing.

What happens? The rookie is shocked by the reaction of others. The rookie is put in his place. The rookie—if learning anything from those hard knocks—begins to realize that sometimes what's offered takes a back seat to when and how it's offered.

Just as wisdom helps the kindergartner adjust and learn to play well with others, it also helps her when she enters high school or heads away to college, when her family moves to a new town, when she enters the work force as an adult.

Wisdom can build on wisdom. If she can remember how being a cocky ninth grader caused her all kinds of problems, she may more readily resist the urge to be a cocky college freshman.

An individual can gain practical wisdom in countless areas: getting along with family members, establishing and maintaining friendships, dealing with personal setbacks, anger, and grief. Dealing with life.

A key to this type of wisdom, as with all wisdom, is knowing that we don't know it all. It's realizing that as we do come to know more and more, we have to accept the fact that there's even more and more we don't know.

Oddly enough, true wisdom requires us to know that we know very little. Then we are very grateful for the smidgen we do know, and are willing and open to learning even more.

In our daily lives, wisdom can be the oxymoron known as common sense: We prize it so highly, or at least always pay it lip service, because it's so rare—and because life is so much harder, so much more complicated, without it.

It's wisdom that gives our life some order, allowing us to prioritize obligations and tasks, focus on what matters, and not become sidetracked by distractions. We are all subject to so many demands—not just on our time, not just on our bodies, but also on our minds, and even on our souls.

In everyday life, wisdom is the gift that lets us correctly determine when to shut off the cell phone and beeper; when to put in the extra hours on the job, and when to leave early; when to do this instead of that; when to do this *before* doing that.

Wisdom is the gift that helps us realize, to borrow a line from G. K. Chesterton, that not everything worth doing is worth doing well. For those of us who lean toward an unhealthy perfectionism, wisdom is the gift that helps us begin to see that, in some cases, good enough is good enough. And for those who like to believe that good enough is *always* good enough, wisdom points out that, in some cases, that isn't so.

To say it again: Wisdom—like all gifts of the Holy Spirit—is very personal. One size doesn't fit all. How one person uses wisdom—how he needs to use wisdom—may be very different from how another uses it or needs to use it.

One person may need to take a few minutes each day to visit with her coworkers, to break out of a self-made shell. Another may need to shut up more often and get more work done. The thing about these gifts of the Spirit is that God gives each person—he gives you, he gives me—*exactly* what we need when we need it and how we need it. What he doesn't do is always give us exactly what we want—when we want it and how we want it.

In other words, we can always have just the right tools, just the right raw material, to make exactly what God wants us to make. And, ultimately and always, what he wants is for us to make ourselves more into his image. That's how we were created and that process isn't complete. Getting the job done is a joint effort: God and you. God and me. God and us.

"Us" because sometimes we're the tool, we're the material, that someone else needs. We're the answer to that person's spoken or unspoken prayer. Another example: A coworker is having a tough time getting along with the boss and notices your approach. She may ask your advice, or she may just start to imitate your style. You are a source of wisdom—not necessarily a font offering specific answers, but an example.

It could be that your coworker never prayed for this gift of the Holy Spirit. It could be that she doesn't believe in God at all. Fortunately, to quote an old saying, that doesn't mean God doesn't believe in her. We don't have to ask for the gifts of the Holy Spirit to receive these gifts. We don't have to believe in the Holy Spirit to receive them, just as we don't have to believe in God to benefit from his gift of life. Still, we can best recognize the true nature of the gift and use it in the best way possible if we *do* believe in the Giver. If we know there is a Spirit and we know he offers these gifts, we'd be foolish not to ask for them, not to beg for them, not to be downright greedy in trying to acquire them. We'd be more foolish not to be on the lookout for them in our own lives, not to use what we have been given, not to take full advantage of the prime sources of the gifts—the church, the sacraments, the Mass, Scripture, personal and communal prayer, service to others—the Giver has chosen to use.

If the gift of wisdom were only available to help with the very practical aspects of our life, it would still be great, still be a treasure. It's more than that because it is spiritual wisdom as well. Thank God.

Spiritual wisdom can be intimately tied up with practical wisdom. A smart-mouthed ninth grader shuts up around the tenth graders because he knows that if he doesn't they will pounce on him, one way or another. Then, too, his being so smart-mouthed could well be a symptom of an unhealthy pride, a sign that he thinks he's better than others. He may shut up because he doesn't want to get pounded, only to discover that shutting up also makes it possible for him to look beyond himself. By closing his mouth, he begins to realize he's not the center of creation, not the be all and end all.

Practical wisdom helps us begin to see that wisdom itself—which comes in many forms and is useful in so many areas of our life—exists. We begin to figure out that this is a virtue we want more of. We want to recognize it in others and take advantage of what they are offering us. We want to cultivate it in ourselves, not just when dealing with day-in, day-out life—school, work, family, friends—but in dealing with the big questions. The hard questions: Who am I? Why am I here? What's life all about and where do I fit in? What comes next?

The gift—recognized, examined, appreciated, and further sought after—leads back to the Giver. Wisdom leads back to the Holy Spirit. And the Spirit has an endless supply of wisdom and boundless generosity.

If our life is a compass, then wisdom is the needle. It orients us, points us in the right direction, and guides us

THE SPIRIT IN THE TRINITY

under all conditions. It turns our face toward the One who wants us to spend eternity seeing him.

On the Flip Side: Fools Rush In

The opposite of wisdom is foolishness.

Practical foolishness leads to trouble. It leads to all sorts of unnecessary complications. Spiritual foolishness leads to sin. It can be the key to despair.

There's a difference between foolishness and inexperience. Both the fool and the rookie suffer, but the fool doesn't learn from that suffering. He makes the same mistake again and again.

Worse, his actions—his attitude—affect not just him, but those with whom he comes into contact. His foolishness is like the cloud of dirt that always accompanied Pig Pen, the Charles Schulz cartoon character who was known for his filth.

We all know fools. We see them every day. Some mornings they stare back at us from the mirror. If there's a motto for fools, it's "Yeah, but . . ." The fool always has an excuse, an often irrational "rationalization" for what he or she does. On the practical level, that person knows A stitch in time saves nine, Don't burn your bridges, Measure twice, cut once—all those pithy sayings that speak the truth. And yet, time and again, he doesn't stitch in time, she burns, they hack blindly. And when confronted about it, the fool's response is "Yeah, but . . ."

It isn't that a fool can't see, it's that he or she refuses to see and to acknowledge the relationship between that single stitch not made and the large tear that resulted, between the flaming bridge and the broken friendship, between the failure to proceed with diligence and the mess that resulted.

Practical wisdom says that, odds are, if you act like a jerk to other people, they are going to act like jerks toward you. The fool responds with, "Yeah, but he started it. She's the one with the problem, not me. They *always* act that way."

On the spiritual level, the fool goes after fool's gold. He knows that in the past, a new car, the latest electronic gizmo, the corner office has brought only fleeting pleasure, but with *this* car, *this* gizmo, *this* promotion, it will be different. Everything will be different. Now, he says to himself, I'll be happy. Completely. Forever.

So the fool pursues those items—in themselves neither good nor bad, simply items—and fails to take the time to think about the big picture. He blows right by opportunities to examine more closely his own life, his own purpose, his own ultimate destiny. He never considers how his relationship with people—rather than with objects—plays a crucial role in that life, purpose, and ultimate destiny.

It's nearly impossible to argue a fool out of her foolishness. Wisdom begins from within, but sometimes it's buried

THE SPIRIT IN THE TRINITY

deep. Still, it's that spark of wisdom, that "Wait a minute here . . . ," that encourages the fool to hesitate, if only for an instant. To consider, if only in passing, that there may be another way. The transformation from foolishness to wisdom is the unfolding of the discovery that there is indeed another way. It's an easier way, ultimately. It's a better way, truly.

How to avoid being a fool? Look for the spark. Pause for the instant. Strive to recognize the truth.

On Wisdom and Foolishness

Wisdom is the foundation, and justice the work without which a foundation cannot stand.

—*ST. AMBROSE (CA. 340–397)*

Whatever you depend on in yourself of wisdom or power, attribute it to him who is the Wisdom and Power of God—that is, to Christ.

—*ST. BERNARD OF CLAIRVAUX (1090–1153)*

There is a great difference between the wisdom of an illuminated and devout man, and the knowledge of a learned and studious scholar.

—*THOMAS À KEMPIS (1379–1471)*

Fools cannot hold their tongue.

—*GEOFFREY CHAUCER (CA. 1342–1400)*

Fools rush in where angels fear to tread.

—*ALEXANDER POPE (1688–1744)*

A Prayer for Wisdom

Come, Holy Spirit, today help me pause. Help me consider. Help me ask for, seek out, and recognize wisdom. As you will, help me be your instrument of wisdom for others who are searching, for others who are hurting. Amen.

CHAPTER THREE

Exit Jesus;
Cue the Holy Spirit
The Gift of Understanding:
When You Get It,
You . . . Get It

The sequel is seldom as good as the original. For the writer Luke, the Gospel bearing his name was volume one and his Acts of the Apostles was volume two.

It couldn't top a Gospel (what could?), but even so, it was and is very good.

Unfortunately, we're so used to hearing the title of this book that we think of it only as the title of this book, almost as if it were one word: *ActsoftheApostles.* But as with any good title, it describes the contents. The book tells of the acts—the adventures, the deeds, the exploits—of the apostles and the early disciples after Jesus ascended into heaven.

As would any good writer, Luke begins his sequel with a recap of the original. *In our last episode . . .*

. . . Jesus did and taught many things and gave instructions to the apostles through the Holy Spirit. He appeared to them for forty days after his resurrection from the dead and talked more about the kingdom of God. While staying—and even eating—with them, he told them to stick around Jerusalem. They were going to be baptized with the Holy Spirit. Soon. Even so, when they met with Jesus near the end of his forty days with them, they just had to ask, "Hey, Lord, now are we going to get serious about giving Rome the boot and restoring the kingdom of Israel?"

They still didn't understand. They lacked a very basic gift.

"Here's what's going to happen," Jesus told them when they were assembled outside town. "The Holy Spirit is going to come upon you and you'll receive power. Then you'll be witnesses here, and in the region, and to the ends of the earth."

Then Christ was lifted up until he entered a cloud.

The Twelve—the Eleven, actually—stood there with their heads tilted back and their jaws hanging open until two men in white robes were suddenly there. "What're you lookin' at?" the pair asked. And then they added, "Jesus is going to return the same way you saw him leave. . . ."

And then Luke continues with part two.

The Eleven returned to the upper room, the one where six weeks ago Jesus had instituted the Eucharist—said the first Mass—and they started praying. There were others present, too—Mary and some of Jesus' relatives. (Sometimes in the

Protestant tradition, they're considered siblings. In the Catholic tradition, the word *brothers* is seen to mean cousins and such.)

Then Peter stood up in front of about 120 people and said that the Holy Spirit, through David, had foretold what would happen to Judas (Psalm 69:25). Now, he continued, they needed to replace him (Psalm 109:8).

It had to be a fellow who had been with Jesus from the time of his baptism by John until his ascension. Two were nominated. The people prayed and lots were cast. In modern-day language, they rolled the dice. Matthias won. From then on, he wasn't just a disciple—a student—but he was also an apostle, a messenger.

Meantime, the group continued waiting and, truth be told, hiding. After all, it hadn't been that long ago that Jesus had been executed. On a Jewish feast called Pentecost (a harvest festival after Passover), the apostles, Mary, Jesus' kinfolk, and some other women were all in one spot, that upper room.

"Suddenly from heaven there came a sound like the rush of a violent wind, and it filled the entire house where they were sitting. Divided tongues, as of fire, appeared among them, and a tongue rested on each of them. All of them were filled with the Holy Spirit and began to speak in other languages, as the Spirit gave them ability" (Acts 2:2–4).

Again, we have the advantage and the disadvantage of two thousand years of reflection and interpretation. But imagine for a moment this event from the apostles' point of view. They had to know God was personal. Yahweh had chosen the Israelites as the people to whom he would reveal more about himself, and he sent them the Messiah, so they weren't unfamiliar with the first person of the Blessed Trinity.

And they certainly knew Jesus, although they didn't quite grasp what he was all about. There was still that undercurrent of "and now we get to be political hot shots." On the other hand, they all knew that they didn't really understand what Jesus was all about or what the Jewish Scriptures—those sacred writings about God's revelation—were all about.

Okay, the Holy Spirit was going to come. Why? Well, because Jesus said the Holy Spirit was going to come, and these witnesses knew two things about Jesus: (1) he didn't lie, and (2) he was always right.

So what were they expecting? These were human beings, after all. They were just like us. Perhaps they assumed the Holy Spirit would be similar to Jesus himself. There would be a knock at the door and someone—Someone— would be standing there. Or, just as Jesus disappeared into the clouds and would someday return that way, the Spirit would arrive from above. Or maybe the Spirit would be born in a manger. But surprise, surprise—and God is always full of surprises—the third person of the Blessed Trinity doesn't enter as a person at all. At least not one who is, like Jesus, fully human and fully divine.

The Holy Spirit is part of the Old Testament and part of the Gospels, but in the Acts of the Apostles the Spirit takes

EXIT JESUS; CUE THE HOLY SPIRIT

center stage. What an entrance the Spirit makes as act 3 begins (act 1 being the creation and fall and God's promise of a savior; act 2 being the Savior's life, death, resurrection, and ascension). Anyone who has heard a serious windstorm approaching knows what Luke means. There's a rumbling in the distance that just keeps coming, just keeps getting louder and *louder!*

In our own time, Luke might have said it was like a freight train approaching. He might have commented that it rattled the fillings in the apostles' teeth. Two thousand years ago there were no trains and no fillings.

But that was what the noise was like and that was how the church began. Pentecost—the descent of the Holy Spirit upon the apostles, Mary, and the others—is seen as the birthday of the church. Yes, obviously, it was centuries in the making as Yahweh prepared us humans. Yes, it was founded and established by Jesus. But it took off—it got its wings—after the Holy Spirit came, just as Christ had promised. And, as it turns out, this Spirit (who didn't knock at the door but, apparently, almost knocked down the door) wasn't really a stranger.

Certainly Mary was familiar with this Spirit from God, this Spirit who *is* God. Some three-plus decades earlier, an angel (the word *angel* also means "messenger") had visited her. He told her she was to be—if she agreed—the mother of the Messiah. "How can this be, since I am a virgin?" she asked.

EXIT JESUS; CUE THE HOLY SPIRIT

The angel answered, "The Holy Spirit will come upon you, and the power of the Most High will overshadow you; therefore the child to be born will be holy; he will be called Son of God."

That's from chapter 1 of the Gospel according to Luke (verse 35). That's right: It's how he began his first book. Luke, by profession a physician, was a talented writer. Scripture scholars point out that among the characteristics of his work is an emphasis on the Holy Spirit and on Mary.

For example, he's the one who tells us that after the shepherds visited the holy family in Bethlehem and told the parents about the angels, Mary "treasured all these words and pondered them in her heart" (Luke 2:19). And it's Luke who included the story about Jesus being lost in the temple at age twelve. Again, he notes that this event, and so many others in Christ's childhood not recorded in his writing, was a memory and an experience that "his mother treasured . . . in her heart" (Luke 2:51).

So it seems safe to speculate that Mary knew who was in that room on Pentecost.

Scripture scholars also point out that Luke's imagery—this tongues-of-fire business—parallels what was used in the Old Testament books of Exodus (19:18) and Isaiah (66:15–20). The author of Exodus describes how Moses brought the people out to meet God and, "Mount Sinai was wrapped in smoke, because the Lord had descended upon it in fire." And Isaiah says "the Lord will come in fire, and his chariots like the whirlwind."

There's a closer, more basic, relationship among the writers of Exodus, Isaiah, and Acts. Each didn't just write about this Spirit, each was inspired by this Spirit.

All authors of sacred Scripture were inspired by the Spirit. Rather than as-told-to accounts, these books are as-moved-by. "God inspired the human authors of the sacred books," says the *Catechism of the Catholic Church* (section 106). "'To compose the sacred books, God chose certain men who, all the while he employed them in this task, made full use of their own faculties and powers so that, though he acted in them and by them, it was as true authors that they consigned to writing whatever he wanted written, and no more'" (*Dei Verbum* 11; cf. John 20:31; 2 Timothy 3:16; 2 Peter 1:19–21; 3:15–16).

We have what we need, in just the right amount, but we have even more than that. We have access to that same Spirit we read about and learn about in those books. That's so because our faith isn't a "religion of the book," but of the "Word" of God—"A word," the *Catechism* (section 108) says, "which is incarnate [made flesh] and living" (St. Bernard, *S. missus est hom.* 4, 11: *Patrologia Latina* 183, 86).

So "if the Scriptures are not to remain a dead letter, Christ, the eternal Word of the living God, must, through the Holy Spirit, 'open [our] minds to understand the Scriptures'" (*CCC*, section 108; cf. Luke 24:45).

That last part of the parenthetical reference wants us to check out Luke ("cf." is an abbreviation for the Latin *confer,* meaning "compare"). Without the living Word, without the Holy Spirit, we just aren't going to get it. We aren't going to understand the words we're reading. We aren't going to understand why those words can be a source of God's gifts to us.

On the first Easter, two gents were heading for Emmaus, a town seven miles from Jerusalem, and chitchatting about all that had happened over the past few days. Then Jesus showed up and walked with them. They caught him up on the conversation and commented that they had hoped this Nazarene now dead—and maybe risen but certainly missing—would be the one to redeem Israel. In Luke 24:25, Jesus replies, "Oh, how foolish you are, and how slow of heart to believe all that the prophets have declared!"

Then Jesus gave them wisdom—the opposite of foolishness. "Beginning with Moses and all the prophets, he interpreted to them the things about himself in all the scriptures" (Luke 24:27).

And they still didn't recognize him, not until dinner and the breaking of the bread, the Eucharist. Then they realized who he was, and he "vanished from their sight" (Luke 24:31).

The duo hightailed it back to Jerusalem and told the Eleven and their companions that Jesus *had* risen from the dead, they had seen him. And "how he had been made known to them in the breaking of the bread" (Luke 24:35).

What is Luke saying? The Scriptures as simply books, as merely words, are interesting, but so what? Without encountering Jesus and, furthermore, recognizing him in the Eucharist, the words never rise above interesting. It's Christ, through the Holy Spirit, who makes them come alive.

"Were not our hearts burning within us," the two asked each other after Jesus had disappeared, "while he was talking to us on the road, while he was opening the scriptures to us?" (Luke 24:32). Jesus later appears to the gathered disciples in Jerusalem, and "Then he opened their minds to understand the scriptures" (Luke 24:45).

Each of us is "on the road." The same Jesus who walked with these two can walk with us. The same Spirit who appeared as tongues of fire over the apostles and the others on Pentecost, the same Spirit who made the two men's hearts burn, can come to us.

Pentecost. Emmaus. Mount Sinai. Such encounters with God—Spirit, Son, and Father—aren't limited to way back when, to someone else. They are possible here and now for each of us.

The Gift of Understanding: When You Get It, You . . . Get It

Wisdom can seem more "spiritual" than simply understanding something for a couple of reasons. One is that wisdom encompasses all the other gifts of the Holy Spirit. It applies to them. It can be the whole package. If you have wisdom and use it, you understand, you seek and give counsel, you strive to increase knowledge, and all the rest.

What we're doing now, beginning with this chapter, is taking that big package and examining the pieces in it. And yet these pieces aren't truly separate from one another. If wisdom is a diamond, the other six gifts are facets of it. If wisdom is a rainbow, the other gifts are the colors that compose it.

For example, wisdom is, ideally, the basis of fortitude, of stepping forward when necessary, of keeping on keeping on. Spin true wisdom in God's light and, sure enough, there are flashes of fortitude. Focus more closely on that rainbow of wisdom, and piety and fear of the Lord are obvious. Wisdom wouldn't be a complete—a truly valuable—diamond without all those facets. It wouldn't be a rainbow without all those colors.

Using a diamond with many facets as an example is an easy, if simplistic, way to explain the gifts of the Holy Spirit. This facet is understanding. That over there is counsel. The rainbow is a trickier, but richer explanation. The bands of the rainbow show how, so often, one color, or one gift, blends into and influences another.

There's a second reason wisdom can seem more spiritual than understanding. Understanding is more "common"; the idea, and even the word itself, is a part of everyday life and language. Then, too, we have seemingly countless ways of asking a person if he or she understands us: "Savvy?" "Ya follow?" "*Capisce?*" "Is that clear?"; and of responding in kind: "You don't have to draw me a picture." "I get it." "The light bulb just went on." "It's crystal clear."

Frequently, when we're asked if we understand, the other person's question involves a concept, an idea or a principle, not simply facts. Understanding is more than knowing the "what"—it's knowing the "why." This gift of the Holy Spirit is the one that sends us on the quest for the whys and helps us find them.

Wisdom can tell us there is a why. Understanding is tracking it down, recognizing it, and then remembering what we've discovered, what we've uncovered, what stands under—supports, holds in place—what? It is remembering every-thing, everyone, and, ultimately and most personally, you.

Let's start "out there" and work our way "in here," since looking closely at ourselves can be a little scary—very rewarding, to be sure, but scary.

So let's talk about physics, chemistry, and biology as they apply to doughnuts. If a fellow eats a lot of doughnuts and doesn't move around much, he puts on weight. He takes in more calories—more units of energy—than he spends and the difference shows up in all sorts of horrible ways in all sorts of horrible places.

If he's an adult, he understands that. He knows the rela-tionship between downing too many doughnuts and standing on the bathroom scale saying "Oh, my!" as his weight goes up. He knows why he shouldn't eat so many doughnuts.

At the same time, he knows that a doughnut once in a while is no problem. A few doughnuts once in a while or a doughnut more than once in a while can be okay. But a lot of doughnuts without that counterbalance of exercise is bad news.

He doesn't need specific knowledge to have this understanding. He doesn't need to know the amount of calories in a maple bar doughnut compared to the amount in a raised glazed doughnut. He doesn't need to know how many calories are burned in a walk around the block compared to the number burned in swimming a few laps in the local pool.

He doesn't even need to know the exact number of doughnuts that is okay if balanced with a certain amount of exercise.

To understand the principle, the why, he need only realize that too many doughnuts combined with a sedentary lifestyle spells some problems. So if he stays on the low side on the intake and on the high side on the outgo, he'll be fine without ever figuring out the exact breakeven point. (Unless, of course, he really loves doughnuts and really hates exercise, and he wants to know the maximum amount of pastry he can eat with the minimum amount of movement.)

So while his actions and the results of those actions involve physics, chemistry, and biology, his understanding is very commonplace. Our lives are filled with and guided by

EXIT JESUS; CUE THE HOLY SPIRIT

ordinary and obvious understanding. Don't step off the roof because . . . Don't stick a fork in a plugged-in toaster because . . . Don't drink and drive because . . . Don't do any of those because—we know—there are very likely and unpleasant consequences of those actions, and we don't want those consequences.

The opposite is also true. There are some consequences we *do* want. We do want to avoid the bad, in whatever form it might take, and so we take certain actions. We brush our teeth. We fill up the car's gas tank before the needle gets to E. We work hard at our job.

None of these things are difficult to understand, once we understand. Then they make perfect sense. None of these have to be taken on faith, although as children we may learn some of them from firsthand experience and as teens we may challenge the validity of a few. But we will never have to try to convince a clear-thinking, healthy adult that "you really don't want to just step off the roof."

This is true no matter what his or her personal beliefs may be when it comes to religion, politics, sex, or dough-nuts. This is true because, somewhere along the line, she stepped off something and fell face first. Or because, as a child, he simply obeyed a parent until reaching adulthood, and then . . .

That's right. He came to understand. Understand what? Gravity exists and it causes certain things to happen. He didn't necessarily learn why it exists or why it does what it does. But even without that knowledge he can understand what it does every time, without fail.

Understanding would be so much easier, "getting it" would be so much easier, if it involved only the stuff that's "out there," like calories and gravity, and if it were limited to such clear-cut cause-and-effect relationships as not putting gas in the car and running out of gas while driving the car.

Where this gift starts to get tricky—and, truth be told, much more interesting and necessary—is in a different kind of relationship: the one between people. Gravity is gravity is gravity. But a coworker is a coworker is a friend is a boss is a . . . Holy smokes! This gets complicated because the people around us are not simply one thing. Ever. We aren't, either, but we'll get to that a little later. Let's focus on them. Again, that can be so much easier and less threatening.

Even as children, we begin to understand the relationship between ourselves and others, between us and a parent. Every kid comes to know when to ask Mom or Dad for something and when to stay quiet. We come to be able to read the signs—storm warnings or sunny weather ahead—and to take appropriate measures.

We all do this. We all learn that every other person is a complicated and often mysterious mix of feelings and worries and joys and all the rest. We see Mom act one way at home, when she is mother, and a different way at Grandma's, when she is daughter. One way in the store as customer, another at work as service provider.

Even as kids, it dawns on us that this notion of multiple roles related to relationships isn't limited to "old people." It's the case even among our own generation. Big brother is this way around us but different around the sister who is older than both of us. Big sister is like this to us but not that way around the kids in the neighborhood who are older than she is. (And—isn't this quite interesting?—at some point both older sister and older brother each suddenly start to act goofy around members of the opposite sex. Hmmm.)

A big part of developing social skills—the ability to play well with others whether in a sandbox or a senior center—is recognizing and understanding how different all those individuals are from one another and also how different any single individual can be within himself or herself. And those differences aren't bad—they're just the opposite. As a human being—a very complicated body and soul—we should have those many layers, those many aspects. As a society—a very complicated mass of beings coming from innumerable experiences and backgrounds—we should have those many variations, those many complementary dynamics.

The person who doesn't understand that this is the case within his or her own circle—family, friends, coworkers, neighbors, parishioners—is the one constantly "stepping off the roof," one way or another. The one who doesn't understand that this is the case within society—beginning with his or her own circle and, truly, encompassing the globe—does the same. In each sphere, the damage isn't limited to self-harm. Others can be hurt, too.

The value, then, of the gift of understanding isn't just knowing that each person is complicated but also understanding *why* he or she is so. The little kid knows Daddy is upset. The wife realizes—or tries to find out—*why* he is.

We have expressions related to this concept. Some old ("Walk a mile in his moccasins"), some new ("baggage"). How do we know what moccasins another is wearing? What baggage she's toting? On first meeting, we probably won't. And it's hazardous to guess, relying on hearsay or stereotyping. Gradually, over time, we reveal more of ourselves to others. We show our true selves even if what we reveal is that we don't like revealing ourselves.

To understand is to pick up on the subtle clues as well as to listen to the blanket statements. It's spotting the body language and inferring the unspoken words.

Ideally, our understanding of another person is grounded in communication. The more I know about you, the easier it is for me to understand you, and vice versa. That doesn't mean we're going to like each other and agree with each other but that we're each going to better understand the other's words, actions, emotions, and beliefs.

Needless to say, that kind of deep communication is extremely infrequent. Too often we rely on mind reading. We think we know what another is thinking or we think we should know what he's thinking. We're seldom correct, and when we are it's probably simply dumb luck. That's one reason the world is such an interesting, confusing, and messy place.

On the other hand, there's no reason for us to know every person to the greatest depth possible. In fact, we can't. We can't even completely understand the one individual we love the most, the one to whom we have pledged our lifelong love. No, spousal mind reading doesn't work.

This doesn't mean we should be discouraged. Just because we aren't able to use a gift to its fullest doesn't mean the gift then has no value. It does. We may not be the best piano player in the world, but if we can really crank out the music, that's a very good thing. We may not be the best teacher in the world, but if we do a great job with our students year after year, we're doing very, very well.

Then, too, we're never going to understand another person completely because that person is constantly changing. It isn't just our experiences from decades ago that shape us; those that happen today can shape us, too. So today we are not the exact same person we were yesterday.

Two examples:

- Someone born in the early 1920s reached adolescence in the middle of the Depression. As a young adult, she and her country faced World War II. Those two experiences, which millions went through, still profoundly influence the people of this generation. Those two major events shape outlooks, perspectives, and priorities.

- This morning, her husband of forty-plus years died suddenly and unexpectedly. She's not the same person today that she was yesterday. Again, her outlook, perspective, and priorities have shifted.

But it isn't just the monumental events—global or personal—that influence us. It's the daily ones, too. The little events are like gentle running water smoothing a rough stone—they are the years spent building a marriage, raising a child, getting an education, or learning a craft.

Then, again, although we are not the same person we were yesterday, generally that difference is less discernible, both to us and to others. Even so, those minuscule differences, which add up and gain weight over time, make a difference in our understanding. And, if they are noticed by others who are aware, they make a difference in how these individuals understand us.

But we aren't blobs. We aren't blank slates. We aren't simply programmed and programmable beings. Because this, this, and this happened to me, I act this way. So then, it's that combination that pops the lock to my—anger, fear, infidelity, mistrust—and there's nothing I can do about it?

No. That personal combination of this, this, and this may give one a leaning toward a behavior, thought, emotion, or belief—a strong leaning. When this leaning is coupled

EXIT JESUS; CUE THE HOLY SPIRIT

with a pattern that has been learned and reinforced over years, if not decades, it can seem that unwanted behaviors, thoughts, emotions, or beliefs are inescapable.

And that might well be true if it weren't for another part of our humanness, another gift from God—free will. We were designed to choose. Why? Because God loves us so much that he decided he would never force us to love him. He wants us to choose him, but we don't have to. He never says, "Love me or I'll send you to hell forever." No, but we can say, "I choose not to love you and I want nothing to do with you forever." We can choose hell. And God says, "Okay."

In big ways and little ways we can tell God to go away and leave us alone. Our power to choose is absolutely amazing. The creator of the universe and the sustainer of all, the One who always is, can be told by you—or me—to scram.

That same personal power, that free will, can be used to overcome the negative baggage we carry: the pain, the lies, the twisting of body and mind (and, at times, it seems like soul, too) that has such a tight grip on us and seems to push us, drag us, goad us, beat us into destructive and self-destructive behavior, thoughts, emotions, and beliefs.

We need to pause here and point out that positive baggage exists, too. The good in our past—the love, the support, the nurturing, the kindness—shapes us, too. It encourages us to love, support, nurture, and be kind.

Obviously, the playing field is not level. One person is raised in an abusive situation or becomes the victim of abuse at some point in those developmental years, and another person never experiences that sort of personal trauma. Both are eyewitnesses; both are being taught how to live.

No one's past can completely match another's, no matter how closely those pasts are intertwined. Consider siblings. What the oldest experienced is different from what the youngest did. They lived in the same house and had the same parents, but there were changes, if only in that the parents had gained experience—understanding and wisdom—while raising the first child that they then used with those who followed. Or rather, using free will, they chose to use that understanding and wisdom.

Free will isn't the only reason we are not trapped by our past. There's also grace. That gift from God—sometimes a spark, sometimes a blaze—is there, can be there, to help us.

Understanding and all the gifts of the Holy Spirit are forms of grace. But what is grace really? The *Catechism of the Catholic Church* has a wonderful glossary that defines it this way:

> The free and undeserved gift that God gives us to respond to our vocation to become his adopted children. As sanctifying grace, God shares his divine life and friendship with us in a habitual gift, a stable and supernatural disposition that enables the soul to

live with God, to act by his love. As actual grace, God gives us the help to conform our lives to his will. Sacramental grace and special graces (charisms, the grace of one's state of life) are gifts of the Holy Spirit to help us live out our Christian vocation (*CCC* section 1996; section 2000; cf. section 654).

"Our vocation" doesn't mean just priesthood or sisterhood, but also our true calling. What is that? Our true calling is God calling us back home, back to him. Our path—how we find our way back—is as unique as we are.

Our discussion has slipped from others to us, from "out there" to "in here." That's the ultimate purpose and use of the gift. It's me understanding me.

In our own time, understanding oneself is the foundation of the formal study of self, the examination of self. It is, as those who know Greek root words have already figured out, the basis of psychology and psychiatry.

Let's take a moment and look at those root words. *Psyche* comes from *psukhe* or *psuche* the Greek word for "breath, principle of life or soul." *Logia* means "the study of." *Iatros* means "a physician."

Seeking the help of a psychiatrist, psychologist, or similar health-care professional can be more than intimidating. It can be downright scary. Too often it's still seen as a sign of weakness. Yes, some cases are more clear-cut than others, but even then there is a tremendous social stigma attached to seeking help for mental health. Mental illness is still commonly viewed with suspicion, fear, and extreme prejudice, even though science has the connection between the physical (the brain itself) and the mental (our thoughts and actions; the mind)—in other words, mental problems have a physical basis.

If our brain isn't functioning properly, for whatever reason, we might see or hear things that don't exist, things that are "only in our minds." We might do things that we otherwise never would.

The brain is so complicated and its physical system of balance so delicate that it can be upset by many things besides mental illness: a very high fever, alcohol or drugs, oxygen deprivation, a physical injury, or a deterioration such as dementia.

Again, these are pretty clear-cut, even though they may develop slowly over time. And again, it's easier—relatively speaking—to understand one's actions, thoughts, and behavior when there is an obvious physical connection. (Prim and proper all her life, the elderly woman in the nursing home now shouts obscenities because she has Alzheimer's disease.)

But what about our normal thoughts and actions? "Why did I get so mad when ... ?" "Why does he just rub me the wrong way?" "Why can't I stop worrying about ... ?" "Why do I do that? I don't want to. I really don't."

We don't understand ourselves. We don't make the connection between what happened way back when and how we behaved this morning. We may not even consciously remember what happened way back when. Or, if we do remember, we may lack the skills to react in a different way, a better way, the way we truly want to act.

Again, here are two examples, this time from my own life. One is pretty silly, the other anything but.

When I was in second or third grade I visited the home of a classmate. We were playing in his backyard when a squirrel scurried by. My friend froze and then headed for the house.

What was this? I had seen countless squirrels and had never given them a second thought except maybe to chase them for fun.

It turned out he was afraid of squirrels. I don't know why. But his action made me reconsider the animals. Maybe there was a dark side to squirrels I knew nothing about. Teeth. Claws. Rabies.

For decades—and I mean decades—I hesitated when a squirrel crossed my path. Sometimes I would think of my former playmate, sometimes not. But, I confess, it wasn't until I was in my forties that it dawned on me that a squirrel had never come after me. A squirrel had never given me a second look except in fear. I had never heard of anyone at any time being attacked—bitten or clawed—by a squirrel.

EXIT JESUS; CUE THE HOLY SPIRIT

My snippet of fear, and my behavior based on it, was groundless, silly, and even amusing.

Example two: Years ago I coauthored a book titled *Speaking Out, Fighting Back*. The author, Good Shepherd Sister Vera Gallagher, had worked in Good Shepherd homes for a long, long time. The teens she had helped—now in their thirties, forties, and beyond—had been contacting her to tell her about their lives.

The sisters made a difference. Their boarding schools were not simply havens for girls who got pregnant, although that was what the public believed (a belief the sisters didn't try to correct because they wanted to shelter the girls in as many ways as possible). No, many of the young ladies under their care were the victims of sexual abuse—perpetrated not just by the stranger in the bushes, but the father, the uncle, the brother, the cousin, the coach, the neighbor, the trusted family friend.

Time and again, these women described to Sister Vera the process of getting their lives back on track and the pivotal roles the Good Shepherd Sisters had played in helping that happen.

After the book was published, other women began to contact her. They hadn't been in any of the Good Shepherd homes, but their lives, their patterns of behavior, mimicked the lives of the women who had been sexually abused. While some could recount being hurt, others had no memory of that happening. Still, by their early to midthirties, they felt desperate; their lives simply wouldn't stay on track—failed relationships, abusive boyfriends, drug and alcohol addiction, poor work and social skills, and a variety of mental, emotional, and physical health problems.

"Why?" they each asked. "Why does it seem so easy for others and impossible for me?"

Our minds, our psyches, our very selves work hard for our survival. For some people, that means burying a single incident or even years of trauma, but that secret takes a toll on the one keeping it. This can occur even if the person is not conscious of the trauma for a long time.

Those women who had no memory of any trauma, of course, are the extreme cases. For them, discovering the why, remembering the what, coming to that self-understanding can carry a high cost. Never discovering and never understanding can cost even more. It truly can be a matter of life and death.

Even if life triumphs, it may be a life—a psyche, a self—that limps, one that, so deeply wounded, will always be influenced by that hurt. Despite that, the person will better understand the why, be better able to live her life accordingly, to see more clearly by increasing her knowledge about herself and about the situation she faced and the fallout from it that she still faces.

How does that discovery and recovery happen? Often through counsel, the next gift of the Holy Spirit. We look at that in chapter 4.

EXIT JESUS; CUE THE HOLY SPIRIT

On the Flip Side: The "-isms" of Bigotry

At the core of any negative "-ism"—racism, sexism, age-ism—is a basic lack of understanding. The bigot just doesn't get it. All too often, the bigot simply refuses to get it. The bigot never grows up.

The child comes to understand that we're all different because _____. Then the child comes to maturity and to the realization that, yes, we're all different, *but* we're all the same because we're all human beings.

That gift ot understanding may be cloaked in human-ism, in a secular outlook or personal philosophy, or in religious beliefs. In any case, understanding is the Holy Spirit at work. (Again, and again, and again: the Holy Spirits leads and guides the church but is not in any way limited to the church. We Catholics—or Christians or believers of any ilk—don't hold the copyright, trademark, or patent on the Spirit.)

But understanding can go beyond that. There can be degrees of this gift. And the step beyond "Yes, we are all human beings" is "It's not just *what* we are, but *who* we are that is priceless."

We all fit into the general category of human being, but within that category are those of a particular sex, age group, race, ethnic heritage, culture, language, set of physical or mental abilities. (How could another's apparent shortcoming help me? By fostering my ability to help another person and forcing me to consider my own shortcomings.)

EXIT JESUS; CUE THE HOLY SPIRIT

Understanding can help us see that what others have—and what we don't have—might just be something very, very good. A lack of understanding causes us to become convinced that what they have—what we don't have—is very, very bad, that how they are different from us is stupid, if not evil.

How does that understanding come about? Most often it comes through one tiny crack in the immaturity. If we're fortunate, immaturity begins to crumble when we're kids—a time in our lives when it's not surprising that we're immature: "Mommy, that man's skin is so dark!" "Daddy, how come she talks so funny?"

One of the wonderful things about that maturity—that deeper, clearer understanding—is that it can begin with one lesson, one incident, one person.

"Well, I've never really known a [Jew . . . Chinese immigrant . . . lesbian] before, but [Samuel . . . Koti . . . Marilyn] is a terrific person." And so the walls come tumbling down. There is a fuller understanding. And even that can increase. Old negative stereotypes are not simply replaced by new positive stereotypes: "All Jews are . . ." "All immigrants are . . ." "All lesbians are . . ."

Rather, just as within my closest circle, just as those with whom I am most familiar, just as it is with any circle, some people are jerks. Or, more charitably, just as within my own circle, within every circle some folks—including me—sometimes act like jerks. This is especially the case in the biggest circle of all: humankind.

EXIT JESUS; CUE THE HOLY SPIRIT

On Understanding and Reason

Understanding is the reward of faith. Therefore seek not to understand that you may believe, but believe that you may understand.

—*ST. AUGUSTINE (354–430)*

Understanding is the sure and clear knowledge of some invisible thing.

—*ST. BERNARD OF CLAIRVAUX (1090–1153)*

Reason in man is rather like God in the world.

—*ST. THOMAS AQUINAS (1225–1274)*

Two excesses: reason excluded, only reason allowed.

—*BLAISE PASCAL (1623–1662)*

Reason can but ascertain the profound difficulties of our condition, it cannot remove them.

—*CARDINAL JOHN HENRY NEWMAN (1801–1890)*

A Prayer for Understanding

Come, Holy Spirit, today allow me to understand more. I want to see as you see, not just others but myself. You live and move and work in each of us. Help me see you. Amen.

EXIT JESUS; CUE THE HOLY SPIRIT

CHAPTER FOUR

Post-Pentecost, St. Paul, and Beyond
The Gift of Counsel: It Beats Flipping a Coin

Let's do a little recap here:

Scripture scholars now point out that the Israelites of the Old Testament were offered a hazy notion of the Holy Spirit and that Jesus, in the Gospels, was much more specific about this . . . what? What exactly was this Holy Spirit? That was the apostles' unasked question as they waited for the Spirit to arrive.

It did arrive, as we saw in chapter 3, and there was a whole lotta shakin' going on. The story continues. And so does the development of this doctrine, even within the New Testament itself: within the rest of the Acts of the Apostles, the book of Revelation, and the Epistles, with St. Paul being the dominant writer of those.

The next step in examining the basics of the Holy Spirit is looking at it through Paul's eyes. Like Luke, Paul was a bright fellow and a man of learning. Yes, he would later work as a tent maker, but his education was grounded in the strict Pharisaic tradition. He knew his stuff.

So what did he know about the Holy Spirit? He certainly knew the rest of the Pentecost story—what happened after the strong wind and the tongues of fire, when all of them in that room were filled with the Holy Spirit. And what does it mean to be filled with the Holy Spirit? They began to speak in other languages as the Spirit gave them the ability (see Acts 2:4).

In chapter 8, we'll examine the gift of tongues (known as glossolalia), but what Luke meant in the Acts of the Apostles is that on that day those who received the Spirit had the ability to speak in a language with which they were not familiar.

At the time, Jerusalem was crowded with visitors, with pilgrims, for the Jewish feast of Pentecost. Many of the people gathered in Jerusalem were near the bull's-eye, that house filled with wind and fire. Though the pilgrims were from a variety of regions with a variety of native languages, each heard the apostles speak in his or her own language.

They were there. They heard the apostles speaking in their languages. They saw the apostles speak to others in completely different languages. They were "amazed and perplexed." "Just what does this mean?" some asked. Others answered, "These guys are drunk." Then, Luke says, Peter spoke up.

First of all, the apostle noted, we haven't been drinking. It's only nine in the morning! No, here's what has happened. Here's what *is* happening.

Then the fisherman, the sincere but cowardly leader of the Twelve, told them about the Spirit and about the Messiah, Jesus, and some listeners were very, very impressed. The works of the Spirit are very, very impressive.

Because that sincere but cowardly fisherman was open to the Spirit, because he accepted the Spirit and allowed himself to be moved by the Spirit, he was transformed. He became the Rock.

Again, it helps to look at all this with new eyes, to pay attention to the story as if we had never heard it before.

The apostles, Mary, and the others wait in the upper room as Jesus instructed them to do. The Spirit comes with wind and fire.

Outsiders—those in town for a holy day but also, most likely, having a bit of a holiday—realize *something* is going on, and they stop to watch the show. Great! Here's a morning's entertainment. There are very odd happenings and a bunch of people yammering away in all kinds of different languages, and, hey, wait a minute, I understand that one over there. He doesn't look like a [Mede . . . Elamite . . . Cappadocian . . . Libyan . . . Roman . . . Cretan . . . Arab], but he sure knows the language. Why, this is more than entertaining. This is downright weird.

Then one of them steps forward and explains what's happening in a way that makes very good sense. And, Luke tells us, those who heard Peter's words "were cut to the heart," and they said to Peter and the other apostles, "What should we do?" (Acts 2:37).

Two things: (1) repent, and (2) be baptized in the name of Jesus so that your sins may be forgiven. And if you do, Peter told them, you'll receive the gift of the Holy Spirit.

Already, immediately, the apostles—the early church—knew that much about the third person of the Blessed Trinity, even though they didn't have those words. The early church would continue to formulate those words—to define the Trinity and look at what that teaching means, based on the Old Testament (the Hebrew Scriptures) and what would become the New Testament. In fact, the New Testament shows that development, both in living a life filled with the Spirit and examining what that kind of life meant—what "the Spirit" meant.

Scripture scholars point out that Paul played a key role in this examination. And Paul pointed out that Pentecost isn't how his story began. He wasn't one of the three thousand (a figure used to mean "a whole bunch") who were baptized on that day. He wasn't one of that core that "devoted themselves to the apostles' teaching and fellowship, to the breaking of bread [the Mass] and the prayers" (Acts 2:42).

POST-PENTECOST, ST. PAUL, AND BEYOND

No, Paul was still Saul at this time, ever zealous, devoted to tracking down members of this group of Jesus' followers and seeing to it that enough rocks were thrown at them that they died a grisly death.

With the teaching of Christ, his real presence in the Eucharist, and the coming of the Holy Spirit, those members of the early church had everything they needed. But that didn't mean their lives were easy or safe. Rome, the occupying force, was against them. The local Jewish authorities were, too.

So for these Spirit-filled apostles and others, there was nowhere to run and nowhere to hide. But because the apostles and others were filled with the Spirit, they weren't inclined to do either, or to stay quiet. Not only did the Twelve preach, attracting crowds, but they shared this Spirit with and healed the multitudes.

In so doing, they were arrested, jailed, beaten. And they just kept going where the Spirit led them. They refused to stop. With the exception of John (who, tradition says, was not martyred), they were killed, one by one.

As that happened, others stepped forward, rushed forward, to take their place, and the church's numbers grew. As Luke points out, the ranks increased because, again led by the Spirit, the early church realized that this message, this way, wasn't meant to be limited to Jews. Jesus, the Messiah, hadn't come just for Yahweh's chosen people.

This broadening of membership doesn't seem like a really big deal for most of us, since most of us don't have a

Jewish background. (Although all Christians have roots in Judaism.) But it was. The tenth chapter of Acts tells how surprised Peter was that a non-Jew would receive the Spirit, that "the gift . . . had been poured out even on the Gentiles" (Acts 10:45). And since that was the case, how could Peter refuse them baptism? He couldn't.

So the Spirit's blowing where it wills wasn't always an easy thing. Just when things seemed predictable, if not comfortable, *whammo!*

Luke includes another instance of the Spirit's unpredictability. Actually, the event is related in chapters 8 and 9 of Acts, just before Peter and the gentiles. Jesus appears to Paul (who is still Saul at this point and has not converted) and asks "Why are you doing this to me?"

What's the connection between the two episodes? The leaders of the church weren't keen on trusting Paul after his conversion. After all, it was their friends and companions whom he had killed. Still, after his conversion they couldn't just turn their backs on him. The solution was that since Paul, filled with the Holy Spirit, wanted to use all of his many talents and his zealous personality to bring others to Christ, he could go out there to the gentiles, go outside Israel.

It wasn't really the church leaders' idea, of course, but they must have seen it as the perfect answer. "While they were worshiping the Lord and fasting, the Holy Spirit said,

'Set apart for me Barnabas and Saul [Paul]for the work to which I have called them'" (Acts 13:2).

And off they went. Paul would make three journeys. Many modern Bibles include a map tracing the routes. What is astounding is how much ground he covered at a time when means of transportation were so primitive. Paul helped establish and got to really know Christian communities over a wide area. And when he wasn't with them, when he couldn't be with them, he'd write those communities a letter. He offered encouragement and praise and gave them a verbal smack on the head when he thought it was needed.

In his letters, Paul would remind them of what he had taught them. And his words, Scripture scholars say, also include a "theology of the Spirit." This theology is more elaborate than what appears in previous books of the Bible, but it's still in the developing stage. In his *Dictionary of the Bible,* John L. McKenzie, S.J., notes that "the Spirit is not obviously and explicitly conceived as a distinct divine personal being in Paul" (844).

So how did we reach the point, in the twenty-first century, that the church could declare and solemnly teach that "the Holy Spirit is thus revealed as another divine person with Jesus and the Father" (*CCC,* section 243)?

Actually, it has been teaching that dogma for a long, long time. Ultimately the answer lies with the Spirit and in the Spirit. It is, it was the Spirit himself who guides the church, who instructs its members in understanding more of what the Trinity has revealed about itself.

The *Catechism of the Catholic Church* notes that the foundation for that teaching is in Scripture. It was the Father and Son who revealed the Spirit. We humans didn't know until we were told. But, as mentioned in chapter 2, it was the Spirit who spoke through the prophets, it was at work since creation, it will be with and in the disciples to teach them and to guide them into all truth.

And "the sending of the person of the Spirit after Jesus' glorification reveals in its fullness the mystery of the Holy Trinity" (*CCC*, section 244). Even so, as the years passed, members of the church, and the church itself as a whole, examined what this meant. Both looked at the relationships within the Trinity and at the role of each Person. As those years passed, there were discussions about the Spirit. There were disagreements. There were fights. Sadly, there were heresies. There were folks who were, the church determined, in error, learned people—some selflessly, some selfishly— teaching something that the church said was not true. And, finally and worse still, there was schism. Christianity split in two. This was long before the Protestant Reformation of the sixteenth century. This break was between the East and the West. That division remains even in our own time.

What was the problem? What *is* the problem?

If you are a Roman Catholic, at every Sunday Mass you state the West's position. What does the "West" mean? The

Catholic Church has nine "rites," what we might call groups, and each has its own particular words and actions for liturgies and the celebration of the sacraments. These include the Byzantine, Armenian, Chaldean, and Coptic. The Roman, or Latin, rite—headed by the pope—is the largest and most dominant worldwide of the nine rites.

Making all this more confusing, the eight other rites within the "Western Catholic Church" can be referred to as the "Eastern Catholic Church." They are "in communion with Rome," accepting the Roman patriarch as the supreme pontiff.

On the other hand, the "East" generally refers to the churches that fall under the broad category of "Orthodox"— Greek Orthodox and Russian Orthodox, for example. They, like the Eastern Catholic rites, trace their origins to four of the original patriarchates: Jerusalem, Antioch, Alexandria, and Constantinople (formerly Byzantium). (The fifth one, way back then, was Rome.) They are not "in communion with Rome"; they don't accept the primacy of the pope.

None of the Orthodox churches match the size of the Roman Catholic rite, but it's important to remember that this isn't about numbers. One side isn't better because it has more members. One side isn't losing because it has less. Rather, it's like a falling out within a family: an honest but devastating disagreement over an important issue, a disagreement that was compounded and made much more complex by many other influences and pressures on both sides.

The church on earth always exists on earth. And on earth none of us, as single human beings or together as a village, kingdom, empire, institution, or other group, are free from many influences and pressures. The church on earth, at any given time, is no exception. Always guided by the Holy Spirit, it's still pushed and poked by secular powers—by politics, by cultures. And those, as we all know, can clash with one another.

When, in the past, the church was closely associated with a particular secular power and that power wanted to exert its influence over others, the church *became* a handy and, at times, effective tool. It *was* used as a weapon.

Obviously, this wasn't right, but, certainly, it happened. Some emperors, kings, and dictators cozied up to the church for the very reason that they could use it as a weapon. When two did this in the same era and they had a falling out, it could be a troublesome time for the church, to say the least.

It's relatively safe to dismiss most of this as ancient history. To all of us nonhistorians it's perhaps vaguely interesting but not too important personally, except, as mentioned a little earlier, if we are a Roman Catholic we state the West's position at every Sunday Mass.

The distinction between East and West was first made by the Roman Empire—there was one leader in Rome and one in Constantinople (now Istanbul, Turkey). At different times in the history of the empire, one of the cities had dominance. In the early church years, it was Rome. Rome ruled. But by the fourth century, the city named for the emperor Constantine had the upper hand.

(Incidentally, it was Constantine who said Christianity was no longer against the law. Actually, it was Constantine and coemperor Licinius Licinianus who issued the Edict of Milan in 313.)

Just what is the Holy Spirit "problem" in all this, then and now? The problem has been, and continues to be, summed up in one word: *Filioque.*

Pronounced FEE-lee-oh-kway, it's Latin for "and the son." "The son" meaning "the Son," Jesus. In the Nicene Creed at Mass, you say the Holy Spirit "proceeds from the Father and the Son." You profess that belief. That's what reciting a creed means. You stand up and declare, "This is what I believe about God: Father, Son, and Spirit. This is what I believe about the church, baptism, sin, resurrection, and eternity."

We'll take a closer look at *Filioque,* its fallout, and the formation of "Trinitarian dogma" in chapter 5.

The Gift of Counsel: It Beats Flipping a Coin

Counsel is tricky because it has two parts. Much of the whole package, the whole gift, hinges on when to turn for help and where to turn for help. Mess up either one and you can be in trouble. Seeking wisdom and attaining understanding, an individual may turn to someone who, apparently, is wiser and understands more. But it ain't necessarily so.

In his first letter to the Corinthians, St. Paul reminds us that there are many gifts but only one Spirit (see 1 Corinthians 12:4–11). He isn't referring to the seven gifts specifically, although he mentions some. Rather, he's focusing on our own individual talents, the things we're good at.

An individual may have wisdom or expertise in a particular area, but be completely incompetent in another. When a person is seeking help in that other area, he or she is best served by seeking out someone who is an expert in that other area.

The seeker also needs to realize and remember that very often this gift—counsel—isn't hand delivered by God. Yes, a gift of the Holy Spirit is from God, but God—divine inspiration or insight—isn't necessarily the messenger.

Two anecdotes, one from a church father (an early theologian), another from a joke book, illustrate this.

About sixteen centuries ago a monk named John Cassian told the fable of two fellow monks setting off into the desert with no food or water. They foolishly ignored common sense, telling themselves, "God will provide."

Later, almost dead from hunger and thirst, they were found by some members of a ferocious tribe. But instead of harming the pair, the bandits offered to help. One monk said, "You bet! Thanks!" The other "refused . . . because it was offered to him by men [not directly by God] and died of starvation."

Both monks made the same stupid mistake. Only one had sense enough to correct it when the opportunity

72

presented itself. God *had* provided, but not in the way either had anticipated.

And the joke: After a heavy rainstorm the river rose quickly and a farmer had to climb onto the roof of his house. A fellow of deep faith, he prayed, "Lord, I know you're going to save me."

Just then a couple of fellows came by in a canoe. "You can hop in with us," they hollered. "No, thanks," he answered. "The Lord is going to save me."

A while later a rescue team in a small powerboat spotted him and pulled up. "Come on, climb in," they said. "Nope," the farmer replied. "God is going to take care of me."

By now the rain had stopped but the water was still rising. A news helicopter buzzed overhead and the pilot got on a loudspeaker. "We can drop a cable and harness," he said, "and can carry you over to dry land."

But the man just shook his head, confident in his Savior.

The water continued to rise, until finally he was caught in the current, swept away, and drowned.

"Lord!" he complained upon entering his eternal reward. "I trusted you. What happened?"

"What happened!" God answered. "I sent a canoe, a boat, and a helicopter!"

It's easy to see that punch line coming. Unfortunately, in real life, it can be harder to see that truth and harder to remember it.

Often another human being is God's messenger. (In which case, he or she really is being *angelic* and *apostolic,* since both words, as we mentioned earlier, come from the Greek word meaning "messenger.") Often another human being is God's answer to our prayers. That's how it is with this gift of the Spirit.

God provides others for us, others who can offer sound advice. There's a catch, of course, but it's not hidden from us. The Spirit doesn't present gifts that include surprises. The whole deal is right there. It's just that sometimes, as we focus on one aspect, one angle, of the gift, we overlook another. We don't see the whole picture.

In the case of the gift of counsel, it's this: God also calls on us to offer sound counsel to others. That's so because, again, receiving the gift of counsel isn't just about receiving something from the Holy Spirit. It's also about giving something from the Holy Spirit to another. God chooses *us* to be his messenger. God chooses *us* to be the answer to another's prayer. It isn't that he *might* do that or that he *can* do that. He *does* do that.

God, in his infinite wisdom and love, chooses *you.* Yes, you. You, singular, reading these words.

No pressure there, right? Suppose you mess up and someone else's life is ruined and it's all your fault and . . .

Easy! Take it easy. It's all going to be okay. Why? Because the gift of counsel means we will be led by the Holy Spirit. It's his gift, after all. And he's going to use it the way he wants.

So what's our responsibility? We must be open to the Spirit, follow the Spirit, rely on the Spirit, just as the apostles were supposed to do when called on to defend their belief in Jesus (see Mark 13:9–11).

So we should just wing it? No. The gift of counsel does not mean we should ad-lib, just grab at straws, or say whatever pops into our brain.

When it comes to the gift of counsel, we have to do the work and we are held accountable for doing the work because God gives us the ability to do the work.

What is that work? It's being open to grace, even while being a member of the "ferocious tribe" (even while wallowing in the selfishness of our sins and being steeped in misery). It's being the one in the canoe, the boat, the helicopter. But, and here we're back to that whole picture of the gift, sometimes we are called to prepare for that role, to begin getting ready even before we know we are preparing, before we realize we have begun.

The Holy Spirit nudges us. Perhaps we have been near death in the desert and, remembering how horrible that was, our compassion wells up and overcomes our greed when we spot those monks. Perhaps we have had the opportunity to learn how to paddle or pilot so that, on a later date, we can be in that craft offering help to another person, offering *the Spirit's* help.

Looking back, it will make sense. Looking back, we will be able to see the path God led us on, the choices he offered,

75

the blessings he presented. (For example, referring again to understanding: The things we learned from those very, very hard times in our life; the insight and the empathy that took seed and root in those tragedies; our own times in the desert or on the roof.)

So let's see if we have this straight. We are supposed to prepare now for what is to come? We are accountable for preparing now for something about which and for someone about whom we may presently know little or nothing?

Yes.

That's a part of this gift. That's at the heart of it, isn't it? We think we're supposed to do this, and we assume that somewhere down the road, there will be a point to it. Some payoff. Someone is going to need exactly what we have to offer at that time and place.

But suppose what we think isn't right? Suppose we prepare and it isn't what we're supposed to be doing? Going back to the flood story, suppose we spent all our time learning how to find people lost in the woods. That's a worthwhile skill but worthless to the fellow stuck on his roof. But this won't happen.

If we are open to the Spirit and his gifts, we will be doing what he wants. God will provide. Not just for the one needing counsel, but also for the one he chooses to provide that counsel. If we are open to the Spirit, we cannot lose.

What does "open" mean? It's being no stranger to the Helper, it's being familiar with the Helper, it's being in love with the Helper and wanting to be his messenger. It's asking for his help and relying on it. It's knowing that Jesus walked on water and welcomes us to do the same. Like Peter we can climb out of the boat and take steps toward Christ. We can take steps that defy all logic and common sense (see Matthew 14:22–33). We can take steps that the Lord invites us to take because he invites us to walk with him.

A couple of things about Peter and Jesus on the water: first, Peter was a fisherman. He knew the water. He knew the boat. Assuming fishermen then were as knowledgeable as fishermen now, he knew that in a storm *you do not leave the boat.* That's still basic watercraft safety. Even if the boat tips over, hang on. Don't try to swim for shore.

If Peter was raised on the water—and it seems safe to speculate that he was, since commercial fishing was his profession as an adult—he probably knew stories of storms and the consequences a fellow faced if he abandoned the boat, whether it was right-side up or upside down. But Peter, being Peter, almost challenged Jesus. "Hey, if it's really you out there, then tell me to come to you."

All right, Peter. Let's take a stroll.

What God asked of him was something that made no sense to him. Still, it was Jesus, and he was asking. He was inviting.

And a second point: Peter's faith didn't last. Not at this point in time it didn't. He became frightened and rightfully so. But when the apostle started to sink, Jesus made sure he was okay.

In spite of all that, later Peter denied knowing Jesus. The cock crowed (see Mark 14:66–72). After spending years with Jesus, after witnessing miracles and being a part of miracles (not just the water walk, but the healing of his mother-in-law, too—see Mark 1:30–31), Peter became scared and made the wrong move.

We all do, time and again. Even as the Spirit prepares us to be counselors, even as we make progress, we get scared. We goof up, and we fail to recognize how the Spirit is preparing us. We fail to trust.

By and large the apostles thought they were being groomed to be little princes in the new kingdom of Israel. This new regime was going to toss Rome out of the land so that they could all live the highlife. But what they were preparing for was something very, very different. It was something much more important: the kingdom of God.

We have similar experiences. We think we are getting ready for this, and then . . . Amazing! We were really preparing for that—"this" being what we thought was the goal, the benefit, the ministry, and "that" being the Spirit's plan all along.

Again, if we are open to the Spirit, if we allow ourselves to be led by the Spirit, it doesn't matter if we think we are preparing for "this." Jesus never said, "Look, guys, you keep harping on this kingdom of Israel stuff, so I'm going to have to let you go."

He, too, trusted in the Spirit.

POST-PENTECOST, ST. PAUL, AND BEYOND

He knew the Spirit would teach the apostles more. And part of that "more" was the realization of what they had already been learning and what they already knew—and where and when and how to offer that wisdom and understanding, that counsel, to others.

Open to the Spirit, we cannot make a mistake. We cannot make the wrong choice. We cannot be unprepared. If we make "Thy will be done" our constant prayer, then we can be confident that God is getting us ready and that we are helping get ourselves ready. (With the awareness that "confident" doesn't equal "cocky." "I'm doing God's will. Me, me, me. All other people, step aside. Here comes God's messenger.")

There's another facet to this gift, another angle: it may well be that what we have prepared for never happens. In sports jargon, we're all set to step up to the plate; we're ready, willing, and able to knock the ball right out of the park; and we spend the whole game in the dugout on the bench.

What? If that happens—when that happens—hasn't the Spirit, well, betrayed us? Hasn't he failed to keep up his end of the bargain? Okay, obviously not, by *why* not?

Because counsel involves three parties: the Spirit and two humans—the Spirit, us, and . . . that third person who has free will. That third person can refuse to accept this gift from the Spirit, can refuse to ask for this gift from the Spirit, and can refuse to even believe in the Spirit.

And so the Spirit's counsel, the Spirit's help, the Spirit's messenger may never get in the game.

The Holy Spirit will not force himself on anyone. God doesn't force us to love him. Ever. He doesn't force us to pray. He doesn't force us to praise him, to thank him, to ask him for help or accept help.

Yes, he does help us whether we ask or not, but we don't have to acknowledge that help, and we certainly don't have to acknowledge the Source of that help. We are perfectly free to deny that the Source even exists. God has great confidence in us and in our ability to choose what is best for us, which, of course, is him.

In the same way, with this gift, we can't go around offering counsel when it isn't wanted. If God does not impose his gifts on anyone, we have no right to. How could we dare even think such a thing?

"Look, God, I know what she really needs to hear, so I'm just going to tell her. I know I'm right, so case closed."

True counsel can't be separated from wisdom. And, as pointed out in chapter 2, a central part of wisdom is knowing when to speak up and when to shut up.

Why can't those gifts be split? All from the Spirit, the seven are so intertwined that each one works in tandem with the others. (In the same way, they aren't given in some rigid numerical order.) One can't be pulled out and applied without the influence and graces of the others. To use a musical metaphor, the gifts are always played together in a chord, they are always in harmony. And if there isn't that harmony, then what we think is a gift or the proper use of a gift isn't so. We're wrong.

The hard-to-take news is that we may never use some aspects of the gift of counsel for which the Spirit has prepared us. This happens when those who could benefit from that gift don't want it.

The good news is that we are not accountable for not using it when that's the case. God calls us to prepare. He doesn't demand that we use the gift. And the preparing alone benefits us—blesses our lives—in countless ways whether we ever use the gift or not.

Then, too, sometimes we do get to use this gift. And what a remarkable sensation that is. It's our own little Pentecost—the Spirit shakes up our soul and our mind. It's an exhilarating and humbling moment because the how and when and why of our preparation become clear. Then we're much like the apostles in that upper room, when Jesus' mission and message fell into place, when they knew, they *really* knew, what he had been preparing them for. And what an honor, what a privilege, it was.

When the Spirit calls on us to offer counsel, there can be a flash of understanding, a realization that we have been prepared for this: this particular area, this particular question, this particular dilemma, this particular fear, this particular pain, and this particular person.

We have the wisdom and the understanding. That's why we're chosen—by God—to offer the counsel.

It's good to keep in mind, too, that how we offer that counsel or receive it may vary. Sometimes the one offering us counsel will do it by his actions and attitude, not by his words. At other times, the person asking for the Spirit's guidance (or seeking it without realizing he or she is asking for it), may receive it from us by our actions and attitude, not our words.

And even when words are used, giving counsel never means being preachy. With or without words, the most effective counsel is offered by what a person is, by what flows naturally—well, supernaturally—from who a person is. What's flowing from one who centers his or her life in the Spirit? The fruits of that Spirit. Always. And in many ways.

What are those fruits? We get both the term and the list from Galatians 5:22–23: "The fruit of the Spirit is love, joy, peace, patience, kindness, generosity, faithfulness, gentleness, and self-control."

When we are filled with God's grace, our heart, mind, and soul are transformed and the fruits of the Spirit grow. An examination of the fruits of the Spirit could fill another whole book, but right now we need to consider a couple of points about the gift of counsel, including a word of caution. We may not even be aware we are offering another person counsel. Someone at work, someone in the neighborhood, someone in the family notices *something* about us. He may ask. He may not. But what we have seems to be what he's looking for.

POST-PENTECOST, ST. PAUL, AND BEYOND

He may get advice from us without our even being aware of it, whether it's through a casual conversation or a comment here and there. Then, too, he may get specific. In either case, we may not know exactly what it is he is seeking. And even if we do, we may not see or know the results. He may never speak of it again. The seed we plant—from the center of that "fruit"—may not take hold for weeks, months, years, or decades.

And we won't have a clue about it, not on this side of eternity.

That's okay. In fact, that's very good for us. Why? Because the reward God offers for the help we gave here will be presented to us on the other side of eternity at Final Judgment. At the end of our earthly life God will judge us, One on one. This is known as Particular Judgment. At the end of time, when Jesus comes again and the world as we know it comes to an end, all of us will face Final Judgment.

Jesus talks about that in Matthew 25:31–46, about separating the sheep from the goats. Members of one group helped him; they fed him, clothed him, visited him in prison, comforted him. Those in the other group didn't. Neither group was aware that it was Christ to whom they were ministering or whom they were ignoring. It seems safe to speculate that one aspect of that ministering, that comforting, was counsel.

At the end of time, we will see the effects of what we did. We'll finally grasp the bigger picture, all the good that came from our relatively simple acts (or act) of kindness and concern.

We will see it and so will everyone else. All humanity will be there.

One more caveat: Let the counselor beware. This gift is meant to be given with a humble and nonjudgmental heart. It demands humility because it's a gift from God to another. We are simply the vessel.

We're not the water satisfying that person's thirst. We're the cup. A cup. A cup God happened to choose. (We also have some choice in the matter. We can refuse to be a cup.)

And counsel demands a nonjudgmental heart because we have no right to judge another. We don't know what's going on in that person's mind, heart, and soul. We can't know what he or she has been through. It's impossible for us to assign a degree of guilt for any particular action he or she has taken.

Fortunately, the same is true about others. They can't judge us. They do not really know us. No one does.

Yes, we can all sit on a jury and vote whether or not we believe a person broke a particular law, but we can't say whether that person sinned. At the same time, sin can't be condoned. It's the nonjudgmental heart that—to use a familiar phrase—hates the sin but loves the sinner (or, more accurately, loves the one who appears to be the sinner).

Much of this chapter has been about offering counsel because, let's admit it, that's what each of us prefers to do. We like to be the one who's wise and understanding; the donor, not the one needing the donation.

But, with this gift, sometimes it's better to receive than to give. Why? Because just as offering counsel can make us lean toward an unhealthy pride, seeking and accepting counsel tends to be, by its very nature, humbling.

Are there any personal confessions more difficult and brutally honest than: I am this way. I don't know how to change it. I can't do it alone.

But if we don't admit those faults, we may well eliminate the opportunity to receive this gift from God, who is using another person to offer it to us.

In our own time, the twelve-step programs are a good example. We don't know how to stop our addiction. We can't do it. We've tried time and again. We've failed time and again. But until we first admit to ourselves that we have this addiction, there's no way we're going to seek counsel, not from another person, not from a group of like-minded people, not from a collective counsel—the practical wisdom—offered by a program.

Once we say, "I am this way," then we can move on: "I don't know how to change it." "I can't do it alone."

There is a progression that leads to receiving the gift. The gift is there. Sometimes we can even see it dangling in front of our eyes. But we have to make that progression to get there. It's humbling, at times humiliating, and, oh, so worth it.

We can't be stupid, either. Alcoholics Anonymous is a good example because its advice is very sound. Unfortunately, some "advice" from other people and programs is bogus. Some does no good at all. Some even hurts the one looking for help.

One of the tasks for the person seeking advice—seeking therapy or treatment—is to examine with a critical eye what's being offered and who's offering it.

To not do this is to possibly become the prey of any variety of snake-oil salesmen, leaders of pseudoreligious cults, or sincere but misguided fools.

Again relying on the Spirit, who's the source of common sense and not just divine wisdom, we need to be careful about who we choose as therapist, counselor, spiritual director, or mentor. The right one can be an incredible blessing.

On the Flip Side: Overdependence and Overindependence

The opposite of counsel comes in two extremes—the far edges of a spectrum on which counsel rests in the middle, like the center of a balancing scale.

At one end is overdependence, that unhealthy clinging to others because of fear or laziness. We take and we take and we take.

At the other is overindependence, that unhealthy refusal to accept another's help even when we need it. Often coupled with that attitude is a refusal to offer help. "I pulled

myself up by my bootstraps and so should everyone else."
Never mind that some folks don't have even those straps.

Then, too, with overindependence can be the willingness to give even while refusing to accept. We don't need anyone's help. We don't need anyone.

Sometimes this overindependence is camouflaged as "family pride." We just don't do that. We don't accept anything we define as "charity." We don't admit we're physically, mentally, or emotionally not well. (Well, all right, we may go to the doctor just before our appendix bursts, but, by God, we won't have anything to do with that namby-pamby, touchy-feely mental health nonsense. That's for losers.)

While being overly dependent is generally looked down on, if not actually scoffed at, the person who is overly independent is the stuff of legends. He or she appears truly mythic. Alone, this rugged individualist accomplished all these things. Alone, this pioneer blazed a trail through a wilderness, whether geographic or otherwise.

Here are two quick reasons why each end of the scale is dangerous:

First, we were created to be social beings. By our very nature we are interdependent. No infant would survive without care, years of care. Throughout our lives, we rely on others in countless ways, and they rely on us.

Second, Jesus not only helped others, but he also turned to others for and depended on others for help, and not just as he grew up. Sometimes it's easy to overlook the fact that the story of his public ministry—the last three years of his life—is the story of the gathering of twelve particular helpers. Yes, he alone, as the Son of God, saved the world. But when founding the church on earth, he immediately began recruiting and training those who would further it, his apostles.

Even a derogatory phrase we use—"Messiah complex"—focuses only on Christ's redeeming of us all. But in his humanity, the Anointed One, filled with the gifts of the Spirit, was neither overly dependent nor overly independent.

He prepared his messengers and he sent them out to practice (see Luke 9:1–6). He taught them and then he left them, confident in the Spirit's work within them. And later he sent out seventy more "laborers into his harvest" (see Luke 10:1–2).

Too often we don't do that when we're in charge of this parish committee or that department at work. We have that twisted Messiah complex and believe not only that we are irreplaceable but also that only our ideas are good and right. The project, the department, will collapse without us.

And doesn't that personal belief make martyrdom easy? Here we are, overworked and underappreciated, as we continue to head the committee—and we don't quite hide our hostility. We still keep a white-knuckle grip on the reins at work—and never fail to point out that we just can't take a vacation. There may be others called by the Spirit to step forward with new ideas, to move in and take over, but we stand in the way.

Maybe there's something else going on. Perhaps the Spirit is telling us it's time to step aside, step down, get out of the way. It's time for us to move on to something new, but as uncomfortable as we are in that familiar position, having to face the unknown frightens us too much to leave it. Maybe the Spirit is saying it's time for this particular committee or project or department to end. It has served its purpose, and the energies and resources now being poured into it would be better used somewhere else. Again, that can be a very scary prospect. Often it takes faith to listen to the Spirit. After all, how can we be sure? Really sure?

We can't. If we could, we wouldn't need faith. In the meantime, we have to rely on the Spirit and his gifts, including the wise counsel of others.

On Counsel

Your choice [of counselor] should be of men approved, not to be proved.

—*ST. BERNARD OF CLAIRVAUX (1090–1153)*

Advisement is good before the deed.

—*GEOFFREY CHAUCER (CA. 1342–1400)*

I have often heard that it is more safe to hear and to take counsel than to give it.

—THOMAS À KEMPIS (CA. 1379–1471)

An honest man may take a fool's advice.

—JOHN DRYDEN (1631–1700)

'Tis not enough your counsel shall be true:
Blunt truths more mischief than nice falsehoods do.

—ALEXANDER POPE (1688–1744)

A Prayer for Counsel

Come, Holy Spirit, today lead me to those with wisdom and understanding. Let me be your voice, your touch, your kindness, your blessing to those who seek your counsel. Prepare me to do your will. Amen.

CHAPTER FIVE

So the Holy Spirit Is, uh . . . Could You Repeat the Question, Please?

The Gift of Knowledge:
Don't Know Much 'bout Much

Christians in the early church had a hard time because, while they knew that they were in possession of the truth, they still weren't quite sure what the truth meant. (The role of the Spirit is an excellent example.) The *Catechism of the Catholic Church* describes the task this way: "During the first centuries the Church sought to clarify her Trinitarian faith, both to deepen her own understanding of the faith and to defend it against the errors that were deforming it" (section 250).

Again, we need to keep in mind that this wasn't just revolutionary. This was, it seemed to devout Jews, blasphemous. God—the one God—was Father. They all knew that, going back to the patriarchs. But now members of the splinter group—those who backed this Jesus of Nazareth—

were continuing to preach Christ. He, too, they said, as the Son of God, was God. The one God.

And, much to the dismay (or maybe even amusement) of the devout Jews, these followers were also saying there was a third . . . What? Not a third God. There was only one God, whole and entire. But there was the Father, the Son, and this Spirit.

How can that be? What can that mean?

The early Christians knew that it was so, even as they realized they weren't sure what it meant. How could they even put such a shocking development—such an astounding revelation—into words?

They had to try, of course, because this was absolutely key to the truth they had been given. It was the foundation upon which their beliefs were based. Jesus, the Son of God, was God. Is God. The Spirit he promised, the Spirit who came, was God. Is God. And so's the Father.

We have to remember that all these things were happening at the same time: the word, the message, was going out. The apostles and others, filled with the Holy Spirit, were boldly telling it to anyone who would listen. And, as Jesus had promised, they were performing miracles, too. They were preaching and baptizing and running the risk of getting arrested, beaten, imprisoned, and killed.

And this fledgling group was beginning to live as a community, with all the hubbub of any group of people coming together for the first time. They had to attend to all the housekeeping items and to the individual personalities that came into play.

Then and there, under those circumstances, the members of the early church had to start clarifying this very basic Trinitarian faith. They had not just to get to the heart of what it meant to be Christian, but to quash any theory they were certain was incorrect, those theories which, naturally enough, some other folks would believe.

"Deformed" teachings began popping up. It's not hard to understand why. Here is a mind-boggling truth, and it's presented to the public. Among those people would surely be some who liked to speculate, to consider, to state with self-assurance.

The same is true today in any general population. Some people just love to have the answers. And among those folks, some just, well, make those answers up. They devise theories that appeal to them or to their sense of logic. And they promote those theories.

That doesn't make those people bad or good. But some people who are bad promote their own theories for their own gain. And some people who are good promote their own theories while not realizing that they are only so much baloney.

So who, in the early church, was going to sort those theories out? Who was going to decide that this is right but that is wrong? That this is correct but that is in error? Or, even more challenging, that this part of that is right but the other part of it is wrong? That this theory contains a degree of truth but also presents errors?

That responsibility, the *Catechism* notes, was the work of the early councils—the meetings of the apostles and bishops. They were helped by the theological works of the church fathers—the early theologians—and they were sustained by the Christian people's sense of the faith.

Historians point out that the first ecumenical—that is, general—council was held in 325 in Nicaea, now İznik, Turkey.

Calling a church council, ecumenical or otherwise, was not a step taken lightly. This wasn't like an annual convention, a perk for management, an opportunity to attend a few sessions and do a little sightseeing, all on the company tab.

Simply getting there, wherever "there" was, meant a long, hard, expensive journey for most participants, even when a generally central location was chosen.

It was the emperor Constantine (d. 337) who convened the First Council of Nicaea. (There was another one there in 787.) Its goal was to resolve the Arian controversy. Arius (ca. 250–336) and his followers said Christ wasn't really God but had been created by the Father to fulfill the Father's plan for salvation. According to Arianism, Jesus was temporal and changeable rather than divine and eternal.

This theory was getting a lot of play in the eastern half of the Roman Empire, and Constantine decided it shouldn't be left in the hands of the local church councils but needed the attention of all the bishops. (Although, getting back to expenses, the emperor footed the bill for the bishops' travel and lodging, letting them use his imperial summer palace.)

At the meeting, an Arian proposed a creed that was rejected. Another statement of belief was offered, this one containing the word *homoousios,* and it was adopted. That Greek word means "consubstantial," or "of one essence," or "of the same substance." Its use was designed to make clear what the church taught about Jesus and his relationship to the Father.

Hard-core Arians didn't buy it, but, over time, the followers of Arius dwindled out.

So, you may be thinking, the Nicene Creed we say at Sunday Mass is the same one that . . . No. The more accurate name for the creed we say is the Nicene-Constantinopolitan Creed, which dates back to the First Council of Constantinople in 381. We'll get to that, and *filioque,* in a bit.

First though, we need to point out that *homoousios* wasn't the only term the early church had to come up with when articulating the dogma of the Trinity. Getting some help from philosophical language, the church also relied on "substance" or "essence" or "nature." And "person," "relation," and *hupostasis* (another word from Greek that came to generally designate an individual instance of a complete, usually intelligent, nature).

The church applied new and unprecedented meaning to that particular vocabulary. From then on, those words would be used to "signify an ineffable mystery, 'infinitely beyond all that we can humanly understand'" (*CCC,* section 251).

How did, and does, the church use these words?

Substance (or *essence* or *nature*) designates the divine Being in its unity.

Person (or *hypostasis*) designates the Father, Son, and Spirit in the real distinction among them.

Relation designates the fact that their distinction lies in the relationship of each to the others.

So . . .

There are three Persons in this one God, the "consubstantial Trinity," to borrow a phrase from the Second Council of Constantinople (553). (Three *Hypostaseis* in one *Ousia* [or substance].)

The divine Persons do not share the one divinity among themselves—each of them is wholly God.

The Council of Toledo held in 675 put it this way: "The Father is that which the Son is, the Son that which the Father is, the Father and Son, that which the Holy Spirit is, i.e., by nature one God."

And the Fourth Lateran Council (held in 1215) said: "Each of the persons is that supreme reality, viz., the divine substance, essence, or nature."

The *Catechism* quotes those councils and then adds: "'God is one but not solitary.' 'Father,' 'Son,' 'Holy Spirit' are not simply names designating modalities of the divine being, for they are really distinct from one another" (section 254).

This type of teaching is hard for those of us not well versed in philosophy or theology. The words seem to start

SO THE HOLY SPIRIT IS, UH . . .

tumbling one over the other, and we aren't sure what they mean. But those words are important. Those teachings, developed over centuries, remain at the core of the Christian faith. That's why it's important to keep trying to clear up our own misunderstanding by adding to our own knowledge.

These three Persons, the church says, are distinct from one another in their relations of origin. The Father "generates," the Son "is begotten," and the Spirit "proceeds." Those were the terms used at the Fourth Lateran Council.

"Because it does not divide the divine unity," the *Catechism* says, "the real distinction of the persons from one another resides solely in the relationships which relate them to one another: 'In the relational names of the persons the Father is related to the Son, the Son to the Father, and the Holy Spirit to both. While they are called three persons in view of their relations, we believe in one nature or substance'" (section 255).

Fortunately, we don't need to understand this in order to believe it. We don't have to be able to explain it. In fact, again, we can't completely understand it. We can't completely explain it.

But that doesn't give us blanket permission to ignore it, either. We do have an obligation to learn more about it, to the best of our ability. And it does have, for lack of a better word, *practical* consequences. Which brings us back to *filioque*.

Using the creed—the profession of faith—from the First Council of Constantinople in 381, we say: "We believe

SO THE HOLY SPIRIT IS, UH . . .

in the Holy Spirit, the Lord, the giver of life, who proceeds from the Father . . ."

But we don't stop there.

The Latin tradition continues "and the Son." Why? It isn't in the original creed. The Council of Florence in 1438 explained that "the Holy Spirit is eternally from Father and Son; he has his nature and subsistence at once (*simul*) from the Father and the Son. He proceeds eternally from both as from one principle and through one spiration. . . . And, since the Father has through generation given to the only-begotten Son everything that belongs to the Father, except being Father, the Son has also eternally from the Father, from whom he is eternally born, that the Holy Spirit proceeds from the Son."

What happened between those councils in 381 and 1438 to bring about such a fundamental change in the creed? Why the gap? Well, during that gap the church split. *Filioque* was one of the central causes of the schism between the Eastern (here that means those now called "Orthodox") and Western Churches. It's remained one ever since.

The *Catechism* admits that "The affirmation of the *filioque* doesn't appear in the creed confessed in 381 at Constantinople." "But," the book immediately continues, "Pope St. Leo I, following an ancient Latin and Alexandrian tradition, confessed it dogmatically in 447." That was before Rome, in 451 at the Council of Chalcedon, "came to recognize and receive the Symbol of 381" (section 247). The use of "and the Son" was gradually admitted into the Latin liturgy between the eighth and eleventh centuries.

The Eastern tradition says the Father's character is the first origin of the Spirit. By saying the Spirit "proceeds from the Father," it means he comes from the Father *through* the Son. The Western Church's tradition first expresses the consubstantial communion between the Father and the Son by saying that the Spirit proceeds from the Father *and* the Son. The Western tradition says it teaches that—again to quote the fifteenth-century Council of Florence—"legitimately and with good reason."

That's because "the eternal order of the divine persons in their consubstantial communion implies that the Father, as 'the principle without principle,' is the first origin of the Spirit, but also that as Father of the only Son, he is, with the Son, the single principle from which the Holy Spirit proceeds" (*CCC*, section 248).

In chapter 6, we'll look at John Paul II's 1986 encyclical on the Spirit.

The Gift of Knowledge: Don't Know Much 'bout Much

A little knowledge, as we all know, is a dangerous thing because if we know a little bit we tend to think we know a lot. And knowing a little isn't the same as knowing a lot.

Most of us can remember when we knew *everything,* or thought we did. Anyone who has raised children or has worked with adolescents has learned that a human being approaching adulthood truly believes he or she knows it all.

He has all the answers. She has everything figured out. Those know-it-alls who are younger are children. Those who are older are hopeless. But then, if that person is fortunate, comes the awakening; or the dethroning. Toppled from that pedestal, the young adult begins to realize how little he or she knows. And that is the beginning of true knowledge.

That is a kernel of truly valuable knowledge.

Apparently, it's always been that way for us human beings. It was the philosopher Socrates who accepted an oracle's description of him as the wisest person in town. Not so, he had first argued, before realizing that perhaps he really was because he was the only resident who at least knew he didn't know anything.

A similar sentiment is often misattributed to author Mark Twain: "When I was a boy of fourteen, my father was so ignorant I could hardly stand to have the old man around. But when I got to be twenty-one, I was astonished at how much the old man had learned in seven years."

Fortunately, God is kind. He allows us to forget almost all the arrogant, self-centered, stupid things we say and do as we approach adulthood. Most of us have only that vague recollection of being know-it-alls. But we can easily spot ourselves—our words and actions—in those younger than we are. In our sons and daughters. In our grandchildren and nieces and nephews. In our students and young neighbors and coworkers.

And we smile. Maybe not on the outside, but certainly on the inside. That is, we smile if what those almost-adults are doing isn't dangerous to themselves or others. If it is, we cringe and advise and pray. A snippet of knowledge really can be dangerous, and each young person must navigate that adolescent minefield alone. There's no other route to adulthood.

As with understanding, it's easy to assume knowledge has nothing to do with God in the way wisdom does. Then, too, a person can be dripping with knowledge and have little understanding and even less wisdom. He can be highly educated but remain horrible at giving or receiving counsel.

It isn't just how we get knowledge, but what that knowledge really is that makes it quite different from the previous three gifts. Generally, knowledge appears to be either rather plain or completely incomprehensible. Much of it can be categorized as "So what?" or "Say what?" Knowledge doesn't have the same reputation—the same glamour—as the first three gifts of the Holy Spirit because the way we receive knowledge is by plodding along.

We all have some of the "So what?" kind. And most of us don't care much about the "Say what?" kind. But just what is the "Say what?" kind of knowledge? That's the type rooted in philosophy. It is the type that can take great delight in turning all thinking—all conventional wisdom—on its head. It's the knowledge gained from the assigned readings in Philosophy 101 that might make us pause and say, "Huh, how about that?" or "This is just plain screwy."

For example, consider the paradoxes of the Greek thinker Zeno (born around 490 B.C.). Among his troublesome offerings are those concerning a race between Achilles and a tortoise in which the tortoise, given a head start, always remains ahead of the fleet-footed runner, and concerning how an arrow in flight can be in only one spot at any particular instant and so can't really be moving to another spot in that instant.

Except, of course, Achilles whups the turtle and the arrow smacks the target.

What does the eighteen year old in the "intro" class really have to know about Zeno and paradoxes. Will knowing this change that person's life? Will it somehow enhance it? No. The information will be filed away in that giant miscellaneous mental box labeled "liberal arts education." Or it will enhance her life because she's majoring or minoring in philosophy.

Even if the eighteen year old never goes beyond Philosophy 101, ideally he or she will be exposed to the idea of examining one's own existence, or at least exposed to the idea that others have examined their own existence. He or she will know that others have questioned and tried to prove or disprove what is real and what is not real, what "real" is . . . and isn't.

For most of us, any interest piqued by Zeno or like-minded thinkers quickly fades because in math or chemistry, and in so many other hard-core "nonliberal" subjects, there is right and there is wrong. And one's grade, and scholarship, may depend on knowing the difference.

Still, there's a value in that philosophical kind of self-examination. There's value in a human being trying to piece together what it means to be a human being as he considers what makes a human being a human being. A large part of what makes us human is the ability to examine our own mind. What other earthly creature does that? What other has that ability?

But the unique ability we have is a gift from God. It is rooted in and basic to what we are. Unless we have a very serious mental or physical disability, each of us is able to gain knowledge. We can learn. And each of us, to one degree or another at one time or another, does a little of that philosophical delving.

Probably we never do it to the degree or the depth that the philosophy major or the philosopher does. But we all do it a little when we ask: "What the heck am I doing? What's the point?"

Even so, generally, when we think about knowledge we don't think about a gift of the Holy Spirit and we don't think about the examined life. We think about the bits and pieces we learned about life itself, starting with those elementary how-tos.

What did we come to know as a small child? What knowledge did we gain? This is how to tie a shoe. This is how to button a shirt so both sides line up evenly. This is our telephone number.

But even before we learned these things, we came to know others. Researchers in human development tell us this,

103

or, rather, they tell us more precisely when in our development we learned that others existed. For instance, we learned that this face—this particular combination of eyes, nose, mouth, chin, ears, and hair—is . . . But we didn't know what to call it then. We weren't able to give it a name because we were preverbal. We had no words. If we did have them, we would have thought, for example, *This is my mama.*

We knew that combination of features. We recognized it. We knew that face. And more than that, we knew what was associated with that face: warmth, food, relief, comfort, love, mother. While, obviously, those abstract concepts were way beyond us as infants, we *knew.*

In our own time, we take a slice of the ancient Hebrews' concept of wisdom—that practical know-how—and give it a different name: knowledge.

Examples of knowledge are looking both ways before crossing the streets; 5 times 5 equals 25. It's those measured steps we take, as we learn more and more. It's those six or eight grades in grade school. In the first grade, if all goes well, a child will learn this, this, and this. In the second, she will learn that, that and that. "That" is built on "this." If there is a shaky foundation of "this," there can be all kinds of trouble with "that."

Some of the basics of this gift have to be spelled out because they *are* so basic. They are so obvious it's easy to overlook them. But the gradual and logical progression of knowledge ties in with the gift. It's central to it.

SO THE HOLY SPIRIT IS, UH . . .

Few of us are blinded by sudden knowledge. We may have an insight we recognize as wisdom. We may connect the dots in a flash of understanding or on occasion hear or give astounding counsel. But, by and large, knowledge doesn't come to us in a single zap. We don't see the whole picture; we're handed the pieces of the puzzle.

So, in a sense, the gift is seldom, if ever, freely and completely given. Rather, it's the opportunity for the gift that is given, piece by piece. Even then, there are strings attached. There are conditions that come with those pieces.

The Holy Spirit doesn't escort us into an elevator and let us zip from the first floor to the penthouse. The Holy Spirit doesn't show us to the escalator and invite us to hop on. He puts us at the foot of the staircase and gives us the opportunity and ability to step up . . . and step up . . . and step up.

That's not to say we do this alone. Always there is God. And, most often, there is someone else.

Let's start with the latter. The vast majority of what we know was passed on to us. Someone knew it before we did—how to tie a shoe; how to correctly button a shirt; how to safely cross a street. Yes, some people are involved in research and such—making discoveries, adding to the general pool of knowledge—but they are the exceptions. Even those discoveries, to one degree or another, rely on previous knowledge that came from . . .

Where?

SO THE HOLY SPIRIT IS, UH . . .

It came from that general pool of knowledge, from that vast collection, which when damaged, destroyed, or lost for a time, can push a society into the dark ages. That, of course, is exactly what happened in the West a few centuries after Christ when the Roman Empire collapsed and countless libraries and schools went with it.

That pool of knowledge, for a time, all but dried up, and the result was horrible. Society stumbled because it quickly forgot so much. The knowledge that had been collected over eras and carefully preserved was tossed onto bonfires. For the most part, those doing the tossing didn't even know what they were doing. They were too stupid—too uneducated—to realize how uneducated they were.

All too soon, there was no one left to tell them what they didn't know. In so many ways, society was back at square one, and it didn't even know there was anything beyond square one. Or, rather, it knew but it didn't know how to move beyond that spot. It saw what previous generations long dead had done—their architecture and engineering, for example—and it didn't know how they had done those things.

Both human sources of knowledge were gone: the people who knew and the written material that contained what they knew. The latter truly was the information the educated shared from beyond the grave, or at least what they had shared until those fires and that destruction.

What does this have to do with us? Some historians point out that the world of today has yet to recover from those times. There are still things that we can see, remnants of the handiwork of those very knowledgeable people, and we don't know how they did what they did.

Even today, experts in certain fields don't know how the ancients did some of what they did.

More personally, those dark ages can point out the central role of another person, many other people, in our own gaining of knowledge. Some of the people who fill these roles are long dead. We rely on their writing and the lessons they taught way back when. Some are still living: the teachers and mentors who guided us from this step to that step, the ones who took what they knew and helped us to learn it.

It's impossible to separate the knowledge we have—this great gift—from those who gave it to us. Without them, we would be very, very ignorant. Without them, the print on this page would be only squiggles to us. The numbers at the bottom of this page would have no meaning. But those symbols do having meaning because we have knowledge in reading and in arithmetic.

We have those skills, we have that knowledge, because of other people. Yes, we worked at it and played a key role in our own education. But—let's be honest—there's no way we, alone, could come up with an alphabet or a numerical system.

Knowledge, then, like love, has to do with community. We receive, we add to, we give. Just as God can love others *through* our loving them, his Spirit can impart the gift of knowledge on them through our actions. As we are loved, we

107

are called to love. As we are taught, we are called to teach, in the broadest sense. Some of us share our knowledge in the classroom; most of us do it outside those walls.

How do we become better at loving God, better at recognizing his love for us? By loving others. How do we become more knowledgeable? By helping others gain knowledge. Was there ever a teacher who didn't discover more about a subject by teaching it? It's the nature of the gift. It's the way it works.

That's why the "other" is so involved in knowledge. There is the other who teaches us and the other who we, in turn, are called on to teach. But, always, in the middle of it is God.

We can't do anything without God's help, but, because he gives us free will, from the very start we get to make some choices when it comes to knowledge. We make decisions not just about our sharing of it, but about our gaining of it. Going back to the image of climbing stairs, we get to decide if we want to contribute to that stepping up, if we want to make the effort.

That single step can be very, very hard. The first day is hard whether we're beginning grade school or graduate school. What's expected at each step, what's presumed of us and our knowledge, is more than what was expected and presumed at the step just below it.

It's that series of very hard steps that takes the student—of any age—from one floor to the next, from one grade to the next, from one degree to the next. When it comes to formal schooling, almost all of us go through that process until we decide we've gone as far as we want to go—or until we're forced to stop because we've gone as far as our particular circumstances will allow.

Then, it can seem, we're supposed to take what we learned in academia and make a living from it. Sometimes the relationship between what we've learned and what we do is obvious. We stayed in school until we had our master's degree in social work and now we're employed as a social worker. Or we went through an apprenticeship program for electricians and now we work as an electrician.

As a society, we tend to be impressed with people who have climbed many steps, who have completed many flights of stairs—those with doctorate degrees in any discipline. We also tend to be judgmental of them.

We look at them with a more critical eye. He has a bachelor's degree in English and he's working at a fast-food restaurant. She was a straight-A student in high school and now she takes tickets at the local movie theater.

Somehow, in our mind, a ton of knowledge is supposed to lead naturally to a heavyweight job. And by that we mean one with prestige: money, power, fame, . . . something!

But the two don't necessarily mesh. They can. A physician—who spent years and years obtaining knowledge—can end up making a tidy income. Another doctor—who is just

SO THE HOLY SPIRIT IS, UH . . .

as smart, studied just as hard, and ended up with just as many school loan debts—may work full-time at a free clinic and may barely scrape by.

So knowledge, then, can be used, can be applied, can be put into practice in many different ways. Most often, one way, in and of itself, is no better than another. Each person, having attained a particular set of knowledge, needs to figure out the correct way to apply it. The choice, the application, is between that person and God. We—outsiders—certainly can't judge. If that person is led by the Holy Spirit—even if he or she doesn't use that expression or even necessarily believe in the Holy Spirit—then the choice will be the right one.

A couple of things to keep in mind:

- God doesn't call us to succeed. Take the free-clinic doctor, for example. She may spend a lifetime trying to get this thing running smoothly and it never does. It never takes root. It never blossoms. It always just gets by, at best.

  Our merciful God may ask her to be faithful to the cause but doesn't hold her accountable if the cause seems to fail. Its success is beyond the scope of her responsibilities. She is only accountable for what she can do.

- Our knowledge isn't limited to what we learn in school. That uptown physician may have his posh practice not only because his patients need only his medical knowledge,

SO THE HOLY SPIRIT IS, UH . . .

but also because he was raised in the upper crust of society and can speak their language. He has the knowledge and experience to hear what is left unspoken and to answer what is left unasked.

It may be that, medical knowledge aside, the rich people rely on this doctor because of their particular needs and the poor people rely on that doctor because of their particular needs. The Holy Spirit, knowing all that, put each physician where each was best suited.

He puts us where it's best.

He offers us the opportunity to gain knowledge—which, again, always takes effort on our part—and then presents us with the opportunity to use and to share that knowledge.

Sometimes our education has nothing to do with our schooling. We learn things we had no intention of learning, things we never, ever wanted to know.

We learn how to be tender, compassionate, present with parents whose young child has died because when our child was young he died. We didn't want to know this. We certainly didn't want to experience this. But because we have experienced it, we *do* know.

Time and again, in every life, there are the "clubs" we are forced to join. There are ones we never wanted to be a member of, never dreamed we'd be a member of, but here

SO THE HOLY SPIRIT IS, UH . . .

we are. And because we are, we have knowledge that can allow us to help new members.

The list of experiences is endless: drug addiction, mental retardation, spina bifida, divorce, sexual abuse, domestic violence, hearing loss, and on and on.

When knowledge from one of these experiences is thrust upon us, it doesn't seem like climbing a flight of stairs. It feels like being shoved down one. More than one. An endless number. And, unlike in academia, we don't know when we'll be done or where we'll be when we're through with a particular "grade."

We simply fall. We simply hurt.

And when we finally seem to stop, to reach the bottom, there are aches that turn into bruises. There are lacerations that turn into scars. There are broken bones that turn into deformities. We have changed. We have been changed forever.

We can't unlearn what has happened. We can try to ignore the experience, but that knowledge—that insider's view, that gut-wrenching lesson or series of lessons—is there.

And where, in this, is God? Where is this all-merciful, all-loving Creator? Where was he as we tumbled, and where is he as we find ourselves in a broken, battered heap?

Again, we learn. We can learn that, at times in our life, God doesn't seem merciful or loving. He doesn't seem to care at all. We can learn that sometimes in the valley of the shadow of death we see only death and not the shepherd. We can learn that we can get angry at God. We can yell at him.

SO THE HOLY SPIRIT IS, UH . . .

We can curse him. We can storm away from him. We can feel betrayed by him.

We can gain all kinds of knowledge we never imagined, never dreamed was possible.

And whether we feel his presence or not, whether we acknowledge his presence or not, God is with us. Theologians may point out that God doesn't create evil or rain down evil, but he allows it as the natural and logical consequence of sin. It's not that we are such notorious sinners that we somehow deserve what has happened to us or to our loved one, but, rather, living in a world steeped in sin, sometimes we or they are its victims.

But those words bring no comfort. We know that. Now we know. Now we know why some people are so angry with God, so angry with the church for what they see as pious prattle, so angry with do-gooders who spout religious adages as if they were talking greeting cards.

We know pain and despair and abandonment because it is what we feel. And because we know it, because we feel it, we can know what another is going through, what another is feeling. In the middle of this horrible mess, the Holy Spirit may offer us an opportunity: the opportunity to use this gift, this knowledge. It's not more than we can handle but what we can handle.

We can do things now that we weren't able to do before our fall. We can do things now because of our fall. And the things we can do, based on what we have learned,

SO THE HOLY SPIRIT IS, UH . . .

can be tremendous. They can be astounding. They can be as powerful as that freight-train-coming encounter on the first Pentecost.

Of course knowledge is power. Its source is our all-powerful God.

On the Flip Side: Choosing to Remain Stupid

Ignorance can't be the opposite of knowledge if knowledge is a gift of the Holy Spirit. No, the opposite has to be sinful in some way. It has to be like the relationship between wisdom and foolishness or understanding and bigotry.

After all, we're all born ignorant. And we all remain that way in most areas of learning. Only a handful come to know a particular field or acquire a particular skill, and they—if they're honest—readily admit that, like Socrates, they mostly know how little they really know.

It's no sin—no fault, no failing—to be ignorant. No, where the responsibility, and even blame, can come into play is in what one does, how one reacts, when presented with the opportunity to acquire knowledge.

Let's go back once again to the Dark Ages. If I am a sincere fellow of normal intelligence who knows nothing of what's in books because I have never seen a book, how can I be at fault?

On the other hand, if I do know and despite that I'm one of the guys who tosses those books on the bonfire, well, then I just might bear some of the responsibility not only for my own lack of knowledge but also for the lack in others.

Let's use a more modern example. If my family cannot afford to send me to college and I cannot afford to pay for tuition myself, am I to blame for not getting a college degree? Have I, in some way, spurned this gift of the Holy Spirit? No.

If, however, the cost of tuition is not a problem for me, and I go to college but never quite get that degree because of, well, beer, pot, laziness, then . . .

In both cases I remain ignorant. I haven't acquired the knowledge that exists. But in one case, I wasn't anywhere near the base of that staircase of learning. In the other, I stood there and refused to climb.

So what's the opposite of this gift of knowledge? In one sense, it's not being ignorant but choosing to remain so. It's also abusing knowledge. If I'm highly educated and I think that means that I'm better than people without an education, I'm dangerously ignorant. Similarly, I'm ignorant if I think that the knowledge I have is all the knowledge I'll ever need.

We always need to be open to the gift of knowledge and to receive the knowledge we're offered as a gift of the Holy Spirit with humble thanks.

On Knowledge

This only I know, that I know not the things which I cannot know.

—*ST. AMBROSE (CA. 340–397)*

Nothing is more excellent than knowledge.

—*ST. JOHN DAMASCENE (CA. 675–749)*

The gift of knowledge makes for the correct management of temporal matters and shows us how to lead good lives in the midst of wicked persons.

—*ST. THOMAS AQUINAS (1225–1274)*

He said he knew what was what.

—*JOHN SKELTON (CA. 1460–1529)*

Knowledge comes of doing. Never to act is never to know.

—*BISHOP JOHN L. SPALDING (1840–1916)*

A Prayer for Knowledge

Come, Holy Spirit, today guide me in the way of knowledge. Help me learn what I am to learn; help me teach what I am to teach. Always help me come to better know and teach Christ. Amen.

CHAPTER SIX

John Paul II on the "Lord and Giver of Life"

The Gift of Fortitude:
Asking the Wizard for Courage

In our own time, three fundamental sources have been written that examine what the church teaches about the Holy Spirit. Not surprisingly, Pope John Paul II played a role in all of them. He was a bishop at the Second Vatican Council, and he helped particularly with the writing of *Gaudium et Spes,* the "Pastoral Constitution on the Church in the Modern World." The *Catechism of the Catholic Church* was written during his pontificate and under his care, although he was not its principal author or editor. And between those two, he wrote an encyclical titled *Dominum et Vivificantem,* that is, "Lord and Giver of Life." It formed the third piece in his examination of the Persons of the Blessed Trinity, joining *Redemptor Hominis*

("Redeemer of Man") in 1979 and *Dives in Misericordia* ("Rich in Mercy") in 1980.

The pontiff later returned to the Trinity in a special way as the second millennium ended (but long before most folks were even familiar with the word *millennium*). He asked Catholics to focus in on Jesus in 1997, on the Spirit in 1998, and on the Father in 1999.

With some thirty-three thousand words and almost three hundred footnotes, *Dominum et Vivificantem* isn't breezy reading. (The complete text is available online at the Vatican's Web site: www.vatican.va.) We should begin with the title itself. Encyclicals—formal papal letters—get their titles from their first words in the Latin text. In English, it begins "The church professes her faith in the Holy Spirit as 'the Lord, the giver of life'"—quoting a phrase Catholics say each Sunday during the creed.

The Spirit, explains the pope in his introduction, is "the one in whom the inscrutable Triune God communicates himself to human beings, constituting in them the source of eternal life." The Spirit is at the center of the Christian faith. It is the "source and dynamic power of the church's renewal."

The encyclical itself is divided into three sections: the Spirit of the Father and the Son, given to the church; the Spirit who convinces the world concerning sin; and the Spirit who gives life.

I. The Spirit of the Father and the Son, Given to the Church

In part I, Pope John Paul II examines John 14. (We looked at that in chapter 2.) This chapter of the Gospel tells how Jesus, on the night before he died, during the Last Supper, promised his apostles "another counselor." The Spirit of truth would be with them—with the church—forever.

That advocate is labeled "another," the pope explains, because Christ was the first bearer and giver of the Good News. This second one—this Paraclete—will teach and let them remember what Christ proclaimed. Those words mean that not only will the Holy Spirit, "in his own particular way . . . continue to inspire the spreading of the Gospel of salvation but also that he will help people understand the correct meaning of the content of Christ's message." He will guide the apostles, and all who follow Jesus (that's us), to the truth.

John Paul II points out that it's characteristic of John's writing that the Father, Son, and Spirit "are clearly called Persons, the first distinct from the second and the third, and each of them from one another." And, "we can say that the highest point of the revelation of the Trinity is reached" in Christ's farewell discourse at the Last Supper.

So at the dawn of the church, just as at the dawn of creation itself, the Spirit is there. Further, "at the price of the Cross, which brings about the Redemption, in the power of the whole Paschal Mystery of Jesus Christ, the Holy Spirit comes in order to remain from the day of Pentecost onwards with the Apostles, to remain with the church and in the church, and through her in the world."

It's after the "departure" of Christ the Son that "the Holy Spirit 'will come' directly (it is his new mission), to complete the work of the Son. Thus it will be he who brings to fulfillment the new era of the history of salvation." That's when, the pope teaches,

> We find ourselves on the threshold of the Paschal events. The new, definitive revelation of the Holy Spirit as a Person who is the gift is accomplished at this precise moment. The Paschal events—the Passion, Death, and Resurrection of Christ—are also the time of the new coming of the Holy Spirit, as the Paraclete and the Spirit of truth. They are the time of the "new beginning" of the self-communication of the Triune God to humanity in the Holy Spirit through the work of Christ the Redeemer. This new beginning is the Redemption of the world: "God so loved the world that he gave his only Son" (John 3:16).

After the Resurrection but before the Ascension, when the apostles were hiding in the upper room, Jesus came to them and showed them his hands and his side. John writes that his words to them were "'Peace be with you. As the Father has sent me, so I send you.' When he had said this, he breathed on them and said to them, 'Receive the Holy Spirit'" (John 20:21–22).

Pope John Paul II explains that Christ "gives them this Spirit as it were through the wounds of his crucifixion: 'He showed them his hands and his side.' It is in the power of this crucifixion that he says to them: 'Receive the Holy Spirit.'

"Thus there is established a close link between the sending of the Son and the sending of the Holy Spirit. There is no sending of the Holy Spirit (after original sin) without the Cross and the Resurrection. . . . The mission of the Son, in a certain sense, finds its 'fulfillment' in the Redemption. The mission of the Holy Spirit 'draws from' the Redemption." (To use a sports analogy, in this relay race, here's where the baton is passed.)

What took place in private on the evening of Easter Sunday became public on Pentecost Sunday. The Spirit—and the church—burst forth.

II. The Spirit Who Convinces the World Concerning Sin

The title the pope uses for part II comes from John 16:8: "And when he comes, he will convince the world concerning sin and righteousness and judgment." Both the individual words and the fact that Jesus linked them in the same phrase are important, the pontiff says.

"Sin," in this passage, means the disbelief that Christ encountered among his own, beginning with the people of his hometown of Nazareth. It means the rejection of his mission, a rejection that will cause people to condemn him to death.

When Christ speaks of righteousness, the pope writes, "Jesus seems to have in mind that definitive justice, which the Father will restore to him when he grants him the glory of the Resurrection and Ascension into heaven: 'I go to the Father.'"

So "in its turn, and in the context of 'sin' and 'righteousness' thus understood, 'judgment' means that the Spirit of truth will show the guilt of the 'world' in condemning Jesus to death on the Cross."

It's important to keep in mind that "convince the world concerning sin" has a broad meaning. "Sin" is all the sins of humanity, not just those faults committed by the first human beings and not just those committed before Christ's life or during it. It's our sins: my sins and your sins.

In those early days of the church, through the workings of the Holy Spirit, Peter began to convince the world concerning sin in his discourse during Pentecost. But we need to remember that this "'convincing' . . . has as its purpose not merely the accusation of the world and still less its condemnation. Jesus Christ did not come into the world to judge it and condemn it but to save it."

"What are we supposed to do?" the crowd asked the apostle. The answer: Repent, be baptized in the name of Jesus for the forgiveness of sins, and you'll receive the gift of the Holy Spirit.

"In this way," the encyclical says, "'convincing concerning sin' becomes at the same time a convincing concerning the remission of sins, in the power of the Holy Spirit. . . . Conversion requires convincing of sin; it includes the interior judgment of the conscience, and this, being a proof of the action of the Spirit of truth in man's inmost being, becomes at the same time a new beginning of the bestowal of grace and love: 'Receive the Holy Spirit'" (John 20:22).

Because of sin we have lost sight of who we are, what we were made for, where we came from, and where we're supposed to end up. But what is sin, at the beginning of creation or as recently as this morning? And what's the relationship between those two sins?

The sin of our first parents—the sin we now call "original"—"is the principal and root of all the others." That sin was humanity's refusal to accept God's invitation to be what it was—what we were—created to be: in communion with God. That sin was humanity saying, "No, God, we're going to decide what's good and what's evil."

Every sin is a refusal. And every time, what we choose by sinning isn't as good as what God offers. We're shortchanging ourselves. But the world has—we have—a hard time believing that. The world needs—we need—convincing. That's what the Spirit does. It's what the Spirit uses the church to do.

And just as Satan was present when the first sin was committed (and he's the one who has already been judged and condemned), he's around today. "The spirit of darkness . . . is capable of showing God as an enemy of his own

123

creature, and in the first place as an enemy of man, as a source of danger and threat to man. In this way Satan manages to sow in man's soul the seed of opposition to the one who 'from the beginning' would be considered as man's enemy—and not as Father. Man is challenged to become the adversary of God!"

On the other hand, "by becoming 'the light of hearts,' . . . that is to say the light of consciences, the Holy Spirit . . . makes man realize his own evil and at the same time directs him toward what is good. Thanks to the multiplicity of the Spirit's gifts, by reason of which he is invoked as the 'sevenfold one,' every kind of human sin can be reached by God's saving power. In reality—as St. Bonaventure says—'by virtue of the seven gifts of the Holy Spirit all evils are destroyed and all good things are produced.'"

This is not to say that we have to accept what's offered us by God. We can refuse conversion, forgiveness, and reconciliation. We can turn down his offer to rebuild communion within humanity and between him and us. We retain the right to "persist in evil"—in sin—and so reject redemption. That is the so-called blasphemy against the Holy Spirit—an unforgivable sin, not because it cannot be forgiven by God but because God's offer of forgiveness is refused by us. It is the "refusal to accept the salvation which God offers to man through the Holy Spirit, working through the power of the Cross."

III. The Spirit Who Gives Life

Pope John Paul II begins his final section by reminding his readers that the reason for the Jubilee of the Year 2000 (then still some fourteen years off!) is this: Christ who was conceived by the Holy Spirit.

Recalling the circumstance of Jesus' birth, he notes: "Mary entered the history of the salvation of the world through the obedience of faith. And faith, in its deepest essence, is the openness of the human heart to the gift: to God's self-communication in the Holy Spirit." And,

> with the mystery of the Incarnation there opens in a new way the source of this divine life in the history of mankind: the Holy Spirit. The Word, "the first-born of all creation," becomes "the first-born of many brethren." . . . And thus he also becomes the head of the Body which is the Church, which will be born on the Cross and revealed on the day of Pentecost— and in the Church, he becomes the head of humanity: of the people of every nation, every race, every country and culture, every language and continent, all called to salvation.

That Spirit "is not only close to this world but present in it, and in a sense immanent, penetrating it and giving it life from within. This is especially true in relation to man: God is present in the intimacy of man's being, in his mind, conscience, and heart" (or as St. Augustine put it, "closer than my inmost being").

We know that "at the culmination of the Paschal Mystery, the Son of God, made man and crucified for the sins of the world, appeared in the midst of his Apostles after the Resurrection, breathed on them and said, 'Receive the Holy Spirit.' This 'breath' continues forever, for 'the Spirit helps us in our weakness.'"

It's our—yours and mine—intimate relationship with God in the Holy Spirit that also enables each of us "to understand himself, his own humanity, in a new way. Thus that image and likeness of God, which man is from his very beginning, is fully realized. . . . This intimate truth of the human being has to be continually rediscovered in the light of Christ who is the prototype of the relationship with God. There also has to be rediscovered in Christ the reason for 'full self-discovery through a sincere gift of himself' to others, as the Second Vatican Council writes: precisely by reason of this divine likeness which 'shows that on earth man . . . is the only creature that God wishes for himself' in his dignity as a person, but as one open to integration and social communion."

The effective knowledge and full implementation of this truth of one's being come about only by the power of the Holy Spirit. "Man learns this truth from Jesus Christ and puts it into practice in his own life by the power of the Spirit, whom Jesus himself has given to us."

The Spirit is the gift. The Spirit is love.

The Gift of Fortitude: Asking the Wizard for Courage

Courage—fortitude—is not the absence of fear. Courage is acting in spite of that fear. Most often when the Holy Spirit comes with this gift he doesn't blow through the house like he did on Pentecost. He uses a tiny voice—whether a person's or one only in our mind—that says, "Go." Do this in spite of all that. Do this because of all that.

And, again, the Holy Spirit, being God, is always overly generous. As always, he doesn't just give us our ration, our portion, but packs it down and lets it spill over (see Luke 6:38). With this gift he invites us, he encourages us, to go, and he goes with us.

It's not like some cowboy movie where one gunfighter says to another, "You make a run for it and I'll cover you." No, he's there every step of the way, not just beside us but inside us. He's there because that's where we need this gift—deep inside. He's there because that's where the fear is.

After looking at what appear from the outside to be some "churchy" gifts, courage seems like a gift everyone would want and one everyone would admire in another.

Every culture, every people, every nation has tales of courage and legendary heroes and heroines. We humans love legends. Some of those stories are from eras and civilizations long past. Others are from today's newspaper. Some are fictitious, some are fanciful, some are fact. Many are a combination of all three.

From the time we're tots—no matter where we're tots—we're told of courage. We are taught to admire it, to recognize it, and to cultivate it in ourselves.

We know the names: David, Mary, Joan of Arc, Maximilian Kolbe, Rosa Parks.

But what is courage, what is fortitude, really? And is getting it truly just a matter of asking the wizard? Are we all pretty much cowardly lions?

All our tales of courage—factual and fictional—have a common theme. They share a common thread. In war movies, it's illustrated by the grizzled combat veteran asking the wide-eyed, untested private, "You scared, boy?"

The lad gulps, straightens up a bit, and manages to squeak, "No, sir!"

"Well," comes the reply, "then you're a fool."

There's a familiar word, one we looked at when we were talking about the Spirit's first gift, wisdom. Courage—even in its most secular, commercial presentation—is closely linked to *not* being a fool.

We could say that acting bravely when one has no fear is just that: acting. On the other hand, true courage can seem like an act to the one who is performing a brave deed. Perhaps cool and calm on the outside, he or she may well be anything but that on the inside.

The person demonstrating the gift of courage may not feel courageous at the time, or even afterward. Rather—again going back to the other gifts—he sees it as something that's right, something that's good—so good that it's worth putting himself in danger. It is so good that he's willing to pay a price, a hefty price, even the ultimate price.

That describes Jesus: the choices he made and his death.

The Gospels tell the story of his love and courage. We focus so often on the first—and we should—that it's easy to overlook the second. But some people were out to get him. They, at times, came after him like a mob. They, at times, conspired to figure out ways to make him trip up on his own words. They, ultimately, enlisted one of his very own, one of his Twelve, to arrange his arrest.

Yes, to quote 1 John 4:18, "perfect love casts out fear," and Jesus loved perfectly. But casting out that fear in order to bring about an ultimate outcome isn't the same as not being prudently fearful of the road—the way of the cross—that leads to that outcome. If fortitude is more than the absence of fear, then Christ relied on this gift of the Spirit. That seems clear in the biblical description of his agony in the garden.

On the night before he was tortured and executed, Jesus prayed that "this cup" be taken away. He didn't want pain. He didn't want his beloved followers to be so frightened and disheartened. He didn't want his mother to witness what was about to happen.

How could he? He was no masochist, no sadist. He knew even Peter—the Rock—would deny him three times and go into hiding (see Matthew 26:34). A dutiful son, time and again Jesus not only helped widows during his public ministry, but from the cross itself he also saw to it that one of his followers would look after his own mom (see John 19:26–27).

Still, what did fortitude give him? It allowed him to understand that God's was the better way, even while knowing what that way included. "Not my will but yours be done" (Luke 22:42). Ultimately, yes, it included Easter and all that has followed from his rising from the dead. But between that Thursday night and Sunday morning . . .

We all have those moments in the garden, those times when we can see pretty clearly—perhaps too clearly—what lies immediately ahead. And we don't want it. Thanks but no thanks. We would prefer to—figuratively or even literally—stay in bed and pull the covers up over our head.

This is so for each of us because each of us must, daily, pick up our cross and follow Christ (Luke 9:23). And when it comes to crosses, most of the time one size doesn't fit all. Just as we each have unique blessings and graces, we each have unique crosses. As individuals, we face challenges—both internal and external—that no one else faces in the same way.

And they just keep coming. They always will in this life, in this world made imperfect by sin and the effects of sin.

We know all this, perhaps too well. Some nights we don't count sheep to fall asleep or take the songwriter's advice and count our blessings instead. No, we slip into counting our worries and our "what-if's," our personal tortures, both large and small, and our concerns not just about ourselves but also about our loved ones.

And sometimes, as we all know, that last cross is the hardest of all—it isn't what we ourselves have to shoulder but what someone dear to us is called on to bear. Then we, like Mary on Good Friday, can only watch, can only be near to, can only pray for that person.

———

We need to pause here for a moment to talk about a medical condition that can seem like a lack of courage. It's one that too often is mistaken for a personal fault: clinical depression.

It, too, can leave one wanting to stay in bed with the covers up over one's head. Even when properly treated through medicine and therapy, it can at times sap an individual not just of her physical strength but of her emotional spirit.

It can drain one of hope, and how can there be courage—the willingness to take on an action, however difficult—where there is no hope, no belief that this difficult task, if undertaken successfully, might lead to better things?

Wisdom is clouded, understanding is skewed, and knowledge is overshadowed when one is in the grip of depression. Then a person must rely more on counsel, trusting the judgment of another even when it seems foolish to trust anyone. If this is not done, sometimes it can seem to the person who is depressed that the only way to put an end to the despair is to take one's own life. In those desperate times, it can be piety that makes the difference, that tips that delicate scale. How so? Because piety is grounded in others. (We'll examine that gift more fully in chapter 7.)

Even if I consider taking my own life and simply telling God I'm sorry and relying on his mercy, or if I come to the point at which I think the hell of the next life can't be as harsh as the hell of my life now, even then there are others to whom I have an obligation and to whom I am rightly devoted: parents, spouse, children, siblings, friends.

And I cannot do this to them.

We began this section speaking of a medical condition that can seem like a lack of courage. The truth is that those who have depression demonstrate extreme fortitude. That's so even when they *do* stay in bed and pull the covers up over their heads.

Their personal cross is a vicious one that can't be seen from the outside. It's one that often can't be articulated by those nailed to it. At most, we on the outside may catch glimpses of their cross through the symptoms we see. They on the inside experience the pain. In the depths of depression, to simply keep on going is an amazing act of bravery.

What if someone doesn't keep going? What if he turns to suicide? Then, as the *Catechism* gently reminds us, "we should not despair of the eternal salvation of persons who have taken their own lives. By ways known to him alone, God can provide the opportunity for salutary [health-giving or beneficial] repentance. The Church prays for persons who have taken their own lives" (section 2283).

Pain is often a part of fortitude. The pain of depression is one kind, but there are so many others. One of the hard parts about pain is that what we're experiencing and how we're experiencing it may be very different from what someone else experiences and how she experiences it.

That's so even at a physical level. We talk of "thresholds" of pain. The doctor asks, "On a scale of one to ten, how bad is it?" But our nine might be his four. Is it because he's tough? Is it because we're weak? There's no way to truly know.

Just as fortitude isn't the absence of fear, it isn't the absence of pain, either. This gift doesn't make us numb. Fortitude can, at times, use that fear or pain as a springboard to lead us to action. There's no denying that fear and pain are great attention getters. Each of us has the ability to focus when we're terrified or in agony.

That's not just human nature; it's the nature of all animals. Fear and pain can drive us creatures, two-legged or four-legged, winged or scaled. But we humans can demonstrate courage and can lead courageous lives even when we aren't under attack or in extreme pain.

Most of us aren't subject to pain and fear for the duration of our lives. Yes, we all face moments. Fortunately, again for most of us, those moments are few. That's what, in part, makes them memorable.

Being rational creatures, having the ability to learn and to reason, we know those moments and challenges will come. If we're honest with ourselves, if we lead any

133

kind of examined life, we know we aren't going to escape pain or fear.

We know we're going to die. That knowledge, researchers have reported, is the ultimate fear. (Although, for some folks, public speaking is a very close second.)

Still, we know we probably aren't going to die today. This morning there are no blips on the personal radar screen. There are no clouds on the horizon. Our health and safety, and those of our loved ones, appear to be secure. For now.

And we're right—given the many days that make up a typical life, the odds of living through the day are in our favor. Given that only a small percentage of people will be victims of violence or accidents today, the odds are in our favor. Given that only so many people out of a vast population will be diagnosed with a serious or even fatal medical condition today, the odds are in our favor.

Yes, today maybe the bad will blind-side me, but most likely it won't.

———

Any discussion of the Holy Spirit's gift of fortitude would be incomplete without talking about the church's martyrs—those men, women, and children who, like Christ, gave witness to their love by giving up their very lives. The apostles and the early followers of the Way had reason to be afraid and to go into hiding after Jesus was arrested. Mary, John, and the loyal women who believed in Christ demonstrated incredible courage when they not only stepped forward but also stepped along with Jesus on his way to Calvary.

The "enemy"—the Romans and the Jewish authorities responsible for his execution—was right there. The authorities could easily have turned on his disciples. (We need to be clear on this: they were responsible for the arrest, sentencing, and carrying out of the sentence. But all humans are truly responsible for what happened. You personally are responsible. Jesus was beaten and killed because you sin. Jesus was beaten and killed because I sin. You are at fault. I am at fault.)

After the Resurrection and the Ascension, after Pentecost, the lives of those who would later come to be called "Christians" were still in serious jeopardy. That would remain the case for the first three centuries because Christianity was against Roman law. It was a capital offense, so those who accepted baptism were accepting a tremendous risk, one that demanded tremendous courage. Nearly all of our early saints were martyrs (a word that comes from the Greek for "witness").

These holy men, women, and children were slaughtered—sometimes for entertainment—because they would not deny that Jesus is Lord, that Jesus is God. In his now famous and often used quote, third-century theologian Tertullian noted, "We multiply whenever we are mown down by you; the blood of Christians is seed."

Some of those early saints looked forward to imitating Christ's sacrifice. They wanted to die for him just as he had died for them: for all of us, for each of us. But it would be a mistake to think that they didn't fear what would happen between the time of their own arrest and that death.

Martyrdom, they correctly believed, leads to heaven. But we sometimes incorrectly believe that their conviction meant they had no fear. They were just like us. (As was Christ: "Like us in all things but sin," says Eucharistic Prayer IV.) They—it seems safe to speculate—worried about the pain. They worried about leaving loved ones behind. They worried about their loved ones' pain, the anguish family and friends would feel from losing someone dear to them, and, perhaps in time, those loved ones' own torture and death.

Even so, as they considered their own Holy Thursday or began their own Good Friday, they never failed to see their own Easter Sunday.

As mentioned before, it was at the beginning of the third century that Roman law changed and Christianity was allowed to exist unhampered. More than that, it was given an imperial boost, which wasn't always necessarily a good thing. (It was on the "in" list and some less-than-sincere folks rushed to join.)

But even since those ancient times, the church has continued to have its martyrs. It has them still, in our own time. We tend to forget that. There are some Catholics in prison today because they're Catholic; some Catholics being tortured or targeted for violence today because they're Catholic; some Catholics being killed today because they're Catholic.

There are members of other Christian denominations in prison or being tortured, targeted, or killed because they are Christian.

Just as the early martyrs' devotion—their true piety—was a source of inspiration and grace for the church of the first centuries, it is also an inspiration for those facing the same harsh treatment today. The blood still flows. The seed is still planted. The same fortitude is given by the same Spirit.

Most of us—thank God—aren't called on to face martyrdom. Most of us, most of the time, don't need the industrial-strength fortitude that a medical or other crisis demands. But many of us rely on a day-to-day fortitude that the particular circumstances of our life demand.

Some among us possess this gift of the Holy Spirit in great abundance and depend on it to make it through just one more day, while the rest of us don't have a clue of what those folks are going through—the coworker taking care of an aging parent, the neighbor praying for a grandchild who's a drug addict, the fellow parishioner waiting to get word back on his son's biopsy, the cousin enduring years of chronic back pain.

Sometimes we know a bit of the story, but it doesn't stay uppermost in our minds because it isn't *our* story.

Sometimes we lend an ear or a hand or a shoulder to cry on, but only for a time.

We don't wake up with it. We don't go to bed with it. We don't toss and turn through the night with it.

We couldn't. We couldn't take on the complete burdens of others. We're not that strong. In the same way, no other person can assume the full weight of ours. We can help; they can help. At times and for a time, we and they can be Simons of Cyrene. But Simon didn't carry Jesus' cross the whole way. He wasn't whipped, mocked, and crucified. He wasn't killed that day.

Our crosses are ours and others' crosses are theirs. There's only so much sharing that can go on, but there's no limit to how much the fortitude we see others demonstrate can help us try to live our life in the same way, to face our fears and pains in the same way, to shoulder our cross in the same way.

Most often, it could be argued, what we admire in others is that day-to-day courage, because that's what's demanded of us, too. It's not so much that we have to step up, although that's true when the "big" demands hit us. No, we just have to keep stepping forward. We have to keep on keeping on. We have to keep being a loving spouse, a giving parent, a dutiful adult child, sibling, aunt or uncle. We have to keep being a responsible worker, a caring friend. We have to keep being good despite all that badness in the world, all the badness that touches us and, at times, seems to attack us and those we love, sometimes viciously, sometimes silently and relentlessly.

We each have a list of personal challenges. "In my life, there is this . . . and this . . . and this"—a divorce, a disabled son or daughter, a life-changing or life-threatening health problem, chronic pain, a split in the family, an awful boss, difficult coworkers, a demanding staff, a horrible or hated job, a crushing financial burden, a loved one addicted to drugs or alcohol—fear, loneliness, misery, grief.

Human life is, at times, the pits—the absolute pits: our life; their life; everyone's life. We need to be very wary of anyone or anything that promises us complete happiness here and now, a happiness that is permanent here and now. It's a lie.

But we get tired, so tired. We get desperate. That's why, again at times, we're fairly easy prey for those who take advantage of weariness and desperation. We turn to embrace this; we rush to buy that.

But it doesn't work. It can't. Whomever, whatever, it is, we can't have complete and permanent happiness. So where's the Christian "Alleluia!" in that dismal belief? Where's the Christian joy?

"Come to me, all you that are weary and are carrying heavy burdens, and I will give you rest," Jesus said. He promised! "Take my yoke upon you, and learn from me; for I am gentle and humble in heart, and you will find rest for your souls. For my yoke is easy, and my burden is light" (Matthew 11:28–30).

So Christ will wipe away our burdens? Or, to use a more contemporary idiom, he will delete them? If so, then we don't have much need for the Spirit's gift of fortitude. If so, then why is it among these seven special graces? Should that list really include only six?

No, we still need fortitude.

So, let's first look at what Scripture scholars say about those verses and then consider them in light of the sometimes exhausting reality of our own daily lives.

When Jesus says, "Come to me," he's speaking as wisdom personified (as in Proverbs 8, which presents traditionally feminine characteristics, offering rest and comfort). It's an offer for all who labor, all who are weary. Jesus, Scripture scholars say, meant the folks excluded by the Pharisees but also probably the Pharisees themselves.

His "yoke" is his interpretation of the Law, the Torah. The people can learn from him. Like them, we are called to be students all our lives, with Christ as our teacher—both the perfect subject matter to study (as the Law personified) and the ideal instructor.

The "rest"—the Sabbath rest—was a symbol for the kingdom of God.

So how is Jesus' yoke easy? Compared to the interpretation of the Law offered by the Pharisees, what Jesus offers is shorter and focuses on what really matters. Even so, because it demands righteousness (see Matthew 5:20), it can also be considered much more difficult. To accept Jesus' yoke is to accept the unlimited requirement of love of God and neighbor.

How does this apply to our lives, to our own weariness and heavy burdens? Jesus invites us to turn to him, to rest with him, by focusing our lives on what really matters. He invites us to toss aside the petty annoyances and obligations and center our time and energy on loving God and others.

But—and this is important—there's no promise of eliminating the crosses and the fears that demand fortitude. If anything, following him adds to our problems. It demands greater fortitude because believing in Christ can turn even family members against one another (see Matthew 10:34–36).

Jesus never promised, and the church never claims, that faithfully following Christ will eliminate the problems we face. Children schooled in Catholicism in the decades before Vatican II were taught this at a tender age in a very early catechism lesson.

Q. Why did God make you?

A. God made me to know, love, and serve him in this world and be happy with him in the next.

A more accurate reply would have been "and be *completely* happy with him in the next." We can find rest for a time now, but only for a time. We will never find, never achieve, never be blessed with complete and unending happiness here and now. That's impossible. That's heaven. And, as we can't help but notice, this isn't.

In this world, in this life, even as we enjoy that brief respite, that moment of God-given peace, we know it's not going to last. But whether at rest or in the thick of things, we're called to continue to learn from Jesus: what he taught and who he was, what he teaches and who he is.

Sometimes that involves education, sometimes prayer, and sometimes the activities—the bumps and bruises, the give-and-take, the joys and sorrows—of our particular daily life and our particular vocation.

We learn on our particular journey home—from this life, with its demands for fortitude, to the next life, where these demands will be replaced by beatitude, that is, complete happiness—that we won't need fortitude in heaven. It will have served its purpose.

On the Flip Side: Letting Fear Dominate

Ask any child what the opposite of being brave is and the likely response will be "Being chicken." But if fortitude isn't the absence of fear, then "being chicken"—if it is the opposite of bravery—isn't really the same as being afraid. So what is it? It's letting that fear dominate. Allowing it to control thoughts and actions.

We're afraid we may run, but running isn't necessarily a bad thing. Wisdom may say, "Head for the hills," and wisdom may speak the truth. But if it's cowardice that's making

JOHN PAUL II ON THE "LORD AND GIVER OF LIFE"

that suggestion, then retreating is the wrong choice and hiding is a mistake.

If fear dominates, we may freeze. We're that deer caught in the headlights. We hope whatever disaster is impending will somehow just go away. We hope we don't have to say anything or do anything. We want to get smaller, to disappear. Our timidity keeps us from standing tall, speaking out, stepping forward.

If fear dominates, we may lie, cheat, steal, or do whatever seems necessary to protect ourselves, even if our actions harm others. Our selfishness and self-centeredness put us above all others. Better they suffer than we do. Let them be the ones blamed. Let them face the consequences. All that matters is our survival or, even more selfishly, simply our comfort.

On Fortitude

The principal act of courage is to endure and withstand dangers doggedly rather than to attack them.

—*ST. THOMAS AQUINAS (1225–1274)*

The brave man seeks not popular applause,
Nor overpower'd with arms, deserts his cause.

—*JOHN DRYDEN (1631–1700)*

Nothing emboldens the wicked so greatly as a lack of courage on the part of the good.

—*POPE LEO XIII (1810–1903)*

Mere physical courage—the absence of fear—simply is not worth calling bravery. It's the bravery of the tiger, not the moral bravery of the man.

—*MONSIGNOR ROBERT HUGH BENSON (1871–1914)*

Courage is almost a contradiction in terms. It means a strong desire to live taking the form of a readiness to die.

—*G. K. CHESTERTON (1874–1936)*

A Prayer for Fortitude

Come, Holy Spirit, today give me the courage to make it through my day. Bless me with fortitude to face the hardest challenges of my life. Help me keep my eyes on Easter. Amen.

JOHN PAUL II ON THE "LORD AND GIVER OF LIFE"

CHAPTER SEVEN

The Spirit and the Sacrament of Confirmation

The Gift of Piety: Nobody Wants to Be a "Holy Joe" or "Holy Jane"

The Holy Spirit is present at all seven sacraments, those outward signs instituted by Christ to give grace, but confirmation has traditionally and appropriately been considered "his" in a special way. (And, of course, so has holy orders.)

The church says confirmation is part of Christian initiation, along with baptism and the Eucharist. Jesus established it when he promised to send the Spirit (see John 14:15–21).

In chapters 3 and 6, we talked about Pentecost and Peter's first address to the people. When they asked what they were to do, he replied, "Repent, and be baptized every one of you in the name of Jesus Christ so that your sins may be forgiven; and you will receive the gift of the Holy Spirit" (Acts 2:38).

Acts (chapters 8 and 19) also tells about a rite that was performed after baptism and that involved the laying on of hands, which allowed the baptized to receive the Holy Spirit.

Still, the early church so intertwined baptism, the Eucharist, and confirmation that it can be hard to distinguish among the three. Typically, they were administered by the bishop in a single rite on Holy Saturday when adult catechumens joined the church.

Then, once again and over time, practices in the East and West began to differ. The East was the first to replace the laying on of hands with anointing. This was seen as "sealing" with the Holy Spirit.

As infant baptism became more common after the fourth century, the East continued to celebrate those three sacraments of initiation together and had a priest administer all of them. In the West, the priest baptized the infant. Communion came later. And then, when the child was older or had even reached adolescence, the bishop confirmed him or her during a pastoral visit.

Because of that separation of the three sacraments, people began to question more what confirmation did above and beyond baptism. It certainly wasn't "rebaptizing." Baptism is a sacrament one receives only once (unlike, for example, the Eucharist), and it's the same with confirmation and holy orders. Confirmation leaves what's called an indelible mark on the soul. It changes a person's soul permanently.

But how does confirmation change one's soul?

THE SPIRIT AND THE SACRAMENT OF CONFIRMATION

Western theologians started to push the teaching that confirmation brings the seven gifts of the Holy Spirit. That was the position of the church fathers, the early theologians. During the Middle Ages, scholars stressed the gift of fortitude. A child nearing or in adolescence was given the strength to fight for the faith.

Historians say this idea was so dominant that a part of the rite itself picked up on it. Older Catholics today may remember a gesture that was part of their own confirmation. The bishop gave the person a slight tap or slap on the cheek. This was seen as a sign that the child had to be ready to lay down his life for the faith. He or she was, upon being confirmed, a soldier of Christ.

In the first half of the twentieth century, that phrase was a rallying cry for the Catholic Action movement. Youngsters entering young adulthood were to be strong and perfect Christians and soldiers of Jesus Christ.

Historians also point out, however, that the tap on the cheek originally didn't have anything to do with "get tough/ be tough." It was really more of what we might call a fatherly caress, a remnant of the sign of peace that was given to those just confirmed.

At the end of the twentieth century, the age at which the sacrament was administered to a child continued to vary, at least in the United States. In some dioceses it was middle school. In others, it was the end of high school. A more universal norm was still being ironed out.

Needless to say, the bishops at the Second Vatican Council wrote about confirmation. "Incorporated in the Church through baptism, the faithful are . . . more perfectly bound to the Church by the sacrament of Confirmation, and the Holy Spirit endows them with special strength so that they are more strictly obliged to spread and defend the faith, both by word and by deed, as true witnesses of Christ" (*Lumen Gentium,* 11).

The Code of Canon Law explains that through confirmation, those who have been baptized "continue on the path of Christian initiation" (no. 879). It's necessary for the completion of baptism's graces, the *Catechism* points out (section 1285).

This doesn't mean we must have it to get to heaven. Rather, it helps us get there.

The *Catechism* also looks at how the laying on of hands, described in Hebrews, became an anointing. In the very early church it was added as a way to show the gift of the Holy Spirit. In fact, the very name "Christian" comes from the Greek for "anointing." Christ was anointed by the Holy Spirit. In the East, the sacrament is known as *Chrismation,* anointing with chrism—that is, perfumed oil. There the oil is also called *myron,* which means chrism. In the West we use the word *confirmation* because it suggests that the sacrament both confirms baptism and strengthens baptismal grace.

Anointing signifies and imprints a spiritual seal. The one being confirmed receives the mark, or seal, of the Spirit, showing that he or she belongs to Christ.

In the Roman rite, the bishop holds out his hands over the ones to be confirmed—a gesture used since apostolic times to signify the gift of the Spirit—as he prays. He prays for the Holy Spirit to give them the seven gifts. The sacrament is conferred through the anointing of the forehead with oil. The priest lays his hand on the person and says, "Be sealed with the gift of the Holy Spirit."

In the Eastern churches of the Byzantine rite, after an initial prayer is said, the forehead, eyes, nose, ears, lips, chest, back, hands, and feet are each anointed with the prayer "The seal of the Holy Spirit."

In either case, the effect is the special outpouring of the Spirit that the apostles experienced on Pentecost. Now, as then, it brings an increase and deepening of baptismal grace. It unites us more firmly to Christ. It increases the gifts of the Spirit in us. It "renders our bond with the Church more perfect" (*CCC*, section 1303). And—to again use the words of Vatican II—it gives us a special strength of the Holy Spirit to spread and to defend the faith by word and action, to be true witnesses of Christ, to confess his name boldly, and to never be ashamed of the cross.

———

Who can be confirmed in the church? Any Catholic who hasn't been. Typically now, with the Rite of Christian Initiation of

Adults, those who weren't confirmed as children or teens receive the sacrament during the Easter Vigil Mass.

And those who are joining the church receive all three sacraments of initiation at that liturgy: baptism, confirmation, and the Eucharist.

Whether a child or adult, the person being confirmed has a sponsor, a spiritual helper. In the past, it was customary to take a confirmation name, a way of asking help from a particular patron saint. That's no longer the case. (If you have not been confirmed and want more information about this sacrament, your local parish could provide it.)

The Gift of Piety: Nobody Wants to Be a "Holy Joe" or "Holy Jane"

The problem with English is that it's a living language. Chaucer and Shakespeare used it, but trying to understand the words of a fourteenth- or sixteenth-century writer takes more than a little effort for most of us in the twenty-first century.

Even what a word commonly meant to most folks fifty years ago isn't necessarily the first definition we think of today. Our not-too-distant ancestors pictured a rodent when someone said "mouse," while we might envision a computer appendage.

That's how it is with the word *piety.*

Wisdom, understanding, counsel, knowledge, fortitude: Okay, we're ready to concede, these are good things. Yes, they're gifts. But *piety?* The Holy Spirit fills a heart, mind, and soul with a sudden urge to kneel up straight? To fold those hands just so? To look and act like some come-to-life illustration from a 1950s holy card?

Dear Holy Spirit: No thanks.

Needless to say, this gift was around long before our negative definition of piety gained so much ground. Even now, when we try to use it in a positive light, it can easily fall flat. "She's very pious." "Oh, that's . . . good," we may respond, even as we think *odd.*

So what is it really?

Since *piety* is derived from the word *pious,* it's better to start there. And it may be best to start with the etymology— the history—of our English word.

Pious comes from the Latin *pius.* You may think that *pius* or the proper noun *Pius*—the name chosen by a dozen popes, including three in the twentieth century—is nothing more than the Latin spelling of *pious.* It may appear to be just an even more holy-holy-holy way to say that someone kneels up straight and so on.

A Latin-English dictionary offers these definitions of *pius:* conscientious, dutiful, God fearing, Godly, holy, fatherly, motherly, brotherly, sisterly, affectionate, patriotic, good, sacred, holy (referring not to a person but to objects associated with religion).

All in all, these are worthwhile traits, but that's the Latin. What about English? An English dictionary defines *pious* this way: marked by or showing reverence for a deity and devotion to divine worship; marked by conspicuous religiosity.

Flipping to the *R*s shows that *religiosity* means religious, but, more specifically, excessively, obtrusively, or sentimentally religious. This could be translated as pain-in-the-neck religious, annoying-to-be-around religious, best-avoided religious.

That doesn't square with true Christianity.

There's more about *pious*. It's also "sacred or devotional as distinct from profane or secular: religious; showing loyal reverence for a thing or a person: dutiful [Good. This is good.]; marked by sham or hypocrisy [Bad. This is bad. And just when things were going so well.]; marked by self-conscious virtue: virtuous; deserving commendation: worthy."

We'll look at a few more definitions and then we'll move on. *Piety* is being pious. It's fidelity to natural obligation (for example, to one's parents). It's dutifulness in religion, that is, devoutness. It can also be an act inspired by piety and a conventional belief or standard (orthodoxy). A synonym is *fidelity*.

All that being said (and it's saying a lot), the negative definitions don't apply when we're talking about the gift. The Holy Spirit would have no reason to make us a pain in the neck to others. (We don't need his help there.)

No, at its core, this gift has to do with our relationship to God and to other humans to whom we owe something. Although it comes in the second half of the list of gifts, it's good to point out its relationship to the first four commandments.

What do they focus on? Our relationship to God and to our parents.

I am the Lord your God. You shall not have strange gods before me.

You shall not take the name of the Lord your God in vain.

Remember to keep holy the Lord's day.

Honor your father and mother.

These four commands can be summed up in two words: be pious.

The message of the first three commandments is to be properly dutiful to the supreme being who created you out of nothing and who continues to sustain you. Why does he do this? Love.

The message of the fourth commandment is to be properly dutiful to those fellow human beings who have given you something for which you can't ever really repay them—your creation, in the case of parents, and your development, in the case of other elders.

We need to pause here for just a moment. Does being pious mean we have to demonstrate deep respect for a parent even if that parent has seriously hurt us by what he or she has done or failed to do? Not at all. Being pious is being *properly* dutiful. It's proper to demonstrate piety toward a parent who truly was a parent in the best sense of the word.

THE SPIRIT AND THE SACRAMENT OF CONFIRMATION

In other instances, Christian charity is always demanded, but isn't piety.

No, piety is the devotion that's appropriate to God and to others. Let's take a look at those others first.

Parents seem an obvious starting point. When we're kids we have no idea of the work and sacrifice it takes to be good parents. After we reach adulthood and we come to learn about the work and sacrifice love demands, we look at our childhood with clearer vision.

It may well be that what we considered ordinary—what perhaps we commonly saw not only in our own family but also in the families of friends—was extraordinary. What seemed natural was rooted in the supernatural. Simply put, we came to know love by our parents loving us.

What's so supernatural about that? God is love. And in his incredible unfolding plan for humanity, he frequently offers each of us the opportunity—in one way or another—to grab hold of the gift of piety and use it. As middle-aged adults learn, sadly and too soon, the roles of parent and child can begin to reverse.

This is not to say that a parent becomes childish or must endure some form of dementia, although that can happen, too. But as the elder's abilities decrease, his or her independence diminishes along with them. Dad can no longer clean out the gutters. Mom can't get to doctor appointments alone. A father, now a widower, needs help preparing nutritious meals. A mother, her eyesight failing, depends on her children to take care of some household chores. It goes on and on.

We can call this filial piety. Forgive me, but I must use a little more Latin here. *Filius* means son. *Filia* means daughter. (*Filioque*, remember?) Caregiving is an act of piety. In fact, that's worth repeating.

Caregiving is an act of piety.

We don't usually think of it in that way because, as noted earlier, we don't commonly have an accurate definition of that gift. But that's what it is and, certainly, that's one of the reasons it's so valuable.

Of course caregiving isn't limited to the parent-child relationship. It can be between spouses. It can be between siblings. It can be between friends. There are endless variations, but in each instance, if we are the one being called on to provide care, then we are also the one in need of this gift of the Holy Spirit. At times, we need a lot of this gift. We need a jumbo-sized version of this gift delivered jumbo-size ASAP. We know that's so because caregiving, which can be an incredible blessing for the giver, can take a heavy toll. Take, for example, the act of caring for an elderly or ailing parent.

Often there is the emotional strain of witnessing a loved one's abilities diminish even as that diminishment puts additional physical responsibilities on the caregiver. We feel horrible as we watch the cancer sap our father's strength even as that increasing weakness means we have to do more for him.

And as a caregiver it can be extremely hard to distinguish—to correctly draw the line—between the feelings of "I have to" and "I am able to." The two aren't always the same.

If the person for whom we are caring regains his or her health, then the "I have to" feeling decreases over time. But if, adding to our distress, our loved one's health isn't going to return, then almost certainly at some point we will be unable to do all that we may feel we have to do, all that we may wish we could do.

Compounding this are our other obligations. For example, in the case of taking care of an aging parent, we may also have a spouse and children. We may have duties at work that are very important. Just because one person needs us and their need is growing doesn't mean that others no longer need us.

Filial piety doesn't require us to burn ourselves out for love of a parent.

As we know, to avoid burnout we may have to say no at some point. So, again, where is the line between those feelings of "I have to" and "I am able to"? Complicating our life even more, that line is not stable. It can shift. It does shift.

But if the Spirit is giving us piety—this proper devotion and, one should assume, the ability to use it—then aren't we falling down on the job if we say no while caregiving? Aren't we, somehow, not using or misusing what the Spirit is offering?

Couldn't we do all that seems demanded of us if only we were stronger, or holier, or a better person?

No. No. No. Not necessarily.

Stop now for a moment and consider Jesus. He's always our model. During his public life, he wasn't constantly "on duty" in the sense that it was all miracles, all healing, all the time. The people sought him out. The people crowded around him. But even so, at times he went away with his apostles. He went away by himself. He rested. (Here's a great line from John 4:6 [the Jerusalem Bible translation]: "Jesus, tired by the journey, sat straight down by the well." The apostles went off to buy food. He just sat there alone until a Samaritan woman came by to get water. He just plopped down and stayed there.)

When Jesus rested, when he went off by himself, was there no longer a need? Had all the people been healed and forgiven? Of course not. People were still blind, crippled, deaf, hungry, and all the rest.

Jesus demonstrated an incredible piety—a devotion—to the people, but piety is not the Spirit's only gift. Now, as then, it's best to see these seven graces as a packaged set. Jesus used that piety wisely. That's what we're to do, too. We're to be wise about our devotion, knowing that as human beings we have limits. We have only so much time, only so much energy.

We need wisdom to understand why a person needing care may ask for more than we can give, why we want to give more then we can give, or even why we don't want to give. We should gain knowledge about our loved one's needs and try to find the best solutions, the best of many choices that can, at times, seem to us and our loved one to be pretty crummy.

We should seek counsel to moderate our piety when that's needed. We should put some trust in a person who can objectively remind us of our limits and gently help us look at our other obligations, including our duty to self. And our duty to self is not to burn out.

Using the example of piety toward one who needs care, we can see how practical the gifts of wisdom, understanding, counsel, knowledge, and fortitude can be and how very necessary they are in our day-to-day lives. And we can begin to acknowledge, not just with our head but with our heart, that a misguided or false piety is no virtue. That kind of devotion—unchecked and quickly out of balance—can cause harm.

We can be alarmed and dismayed to discover that without a pious attitude there can't be truly pious action. We can go through the motions, but it's a sham. And that very thin veneer is quickly stripped away.

We'll get to God and piety in a moment, but first we need to glance at devotion to one's country. To a certain degree, all that we've already said applies. But because there is less emotion between person and country than between person and parent (or spouse or sibling or other loved one), it's a little easier to see the limits.

It's easier to acknowledge that, in some cases, piety isn't appropriate—if, for example, our country's government is corrupt. Then it would make sense to work toward changing it but not to simply promote it or help it as it currently exists.

But while filial and patriotic piety always include that "maybe," piety toward God doesn't work that way. It is *always* proper to show devotion to God.

Why? Because God is perfect. Because God is the supreme being.

The Creator has revealed to his creatures that they are to consider him a parent and that, having become a creature himself (while remaining God), he can be looked upon—in the person of the Son—as a brother.

A very pale comparison would be if we were invited to dine with the most powerful fellow on earth. He meets us at the door, welcomes us to his table, and makes us feel completely at ease. There's no standing on ceremony here. We're with a dear friend.

Even so, just because we are at ease, just because he has done such a great job making us feel welcome, doesn't change the fact that he is the most powerful person on earth. It's hard to believe we would forget that, at least for very long. It seems safe to assume that we would demonstrate a certain amount of respect because of who he is.

We do the same with God—who is our Father, who is our brother Jesus, who is the Spirit of love between them—because he is God. We are not now, and never will be, God's peers, God's equals. And if we keep that in mind, if we cultivate a pious attitude, then it's easier for us to remember a very important truth: The world doesn't revolve around us.

We were created. He always was, always is, and always will be.

He is more than we can ever imagine. And, incredibly, he loves each of us more than we will ever know. And that's why—common sense alone dictates—he deserves respect, at the absolute minimum.

Piety toward God isn't about kneeling up straight, about folding one's hands just so (though those can be indications of piety). It's about acknowledging the relationship between the Creator and the creature. It's about coming to better recognize the Creator's handiwork and presence in all things.

Being pious doesn't mean we say "thee" and "thou" when we pray. Being pious means we turn what we say and do into prayer. We don't create the false categories of "religion" and "real life." We begin to accept the gifts the Holy Spirit offers us in this life and to praise the Source of life.

Just as filial piety and patriotic piety give us opportunities to show our gratitude to parent and country, piety toward God can become a way of living our gratitude. How? Endless hours on our knees in the chapel? Maybe so, if we're a cloistered nun, but it's less likely if we're a soccer mom. In either case, as in the life of Jesus, piety demands a balance between action and contemplation, between work and prayer (in the traditional sense of the word), between time in service to others and time alone with God, between action and rest.

Both action and rest can be pious acts. Why? Because God made us individuals. One of life's greatest challenges (and, truth be told, one aspect that makes it *very* interesting) is discovering—and constantly rediscovering—one's vocation, the path God calls each of us to walk as we journey home to him.

As outsiders, we can't determine very accurately when another person has piety. We can be pretty sure, sometimes, because the pious person will typically exhibit the fruits of the Holy Spirit. (We talked about those in chapter 4.) But because the use of this gift is so closely related to attitude, we just can't tell, from the outside if a person has it.

From the inside, however, it's a different matter.

If we begin to develop the habit of doing things in a pious way—simply put, if we do them because we love God, who deserves all our love—then when that piety is missing, for whatever reason, we notice it.

And because this gift is good—of course it is; all the gifts of the Holy Spirit are good—then we're going to miss it. We're going to want it back. How do we get it? The Holy Spirit continually offers it to us, and, again, through our attitude and our actions we are given the opportunity to receive it.

More than that, it can grow. We can become more pious. We can let piety more strongly influence our life.

THE SPIRIT AND THE SACRAMENT OF CONFIRMATION

When we speak of someone being holy—in the best sense of *that* word—we are speaking of his or her piety.

Why would we want piety in our life? Why would we want to become a pious person? The simplest and most basic reason is that we want to live correctly. We want to live in the manner in which God intended, if only for our own sake. That isn't being selfish or self-centered; it's being practical.

It is best—it is easiest and most advantageous—to use a tool for the purpose and in the manner for which it was intended. A screwdriver works better than a table knife to remove a screw. A table knife works better than a screwdriver to butter a biscuit. Yes, each can be used for both purposes, but that isn't the best use of them.

In a sense, the same is true with us. There is a logical, a natural (or supernatural), basis for showing devotion to the people who deserve our devotion, to the ones we owe, even if those people never call in "our markers."

But, more than that, above and beyond that, it benefits us to do what is right. We are blessed, we receive grace (more of God's life within us), when we do that. Why? Once again, it's because of our extravagant God. He simply can't be outdone.

However much we give, in any arena at any time, and no matter how much we love, he gives us more. He loves us more. This is not to say that his love for us increases. It can't. Infinite love can't get bigger. But our ability to recognize that love, to appreciate that love, can grow tremendously.

THE SPIRIT AND THE SACRAMENT OF CONFIRMATION

Of course, the more that this happens, the more we realize that our devotion to God, our piety, can never come close to what it should be. It's like knowledge—the more we know, the more we know we don't know. Greater piety shows us how little piety we offer compared to what is deserved.

God rightly deserves it all because he's given us everything we have, everything we are, and everything we ever will have or will be.

He's given us life. He's given us knowledge of himself. He's given us his only Son, who died for us. He's given us the Spirit of love between the Father and the Son to help us find our way home to him.

That's a debt we can't repay, but, of course, God doesn't ask that we balance the ledger. His kindness and mercy erase a lot of red ink.

We don't have to settle up—thank God—but we are called on to . . . what? We are called to make token payments (to continue the metaphor), give from our substance and not just our surplus, knowing that our heavenly Father—no matter how much we give—will always keep replacing it with even more.

On the Flip Side: Squandering One's Life

What's the opposite of piety? More than simply a lack of devotion, it's a squandering of the gifts that one's been given.

A classic example of impiety is the prodigal son. You know the story, from Luke 15:11–32. Rich kid wants his inheritance early, goes and blows it, and comes home and apologizes, and Dad welcomes him back into the household.

What you may not realize is what *prodigal* really means. It doesn't have to do with the running away but with the reckless spending. *Prodigal* means foolishly extravagant.

We take what another gives us and we squander it lickety-split.

If we're an eight year old, we take that five dollars Grandma sent for our birthday and run down to the store and get all the candy possible. Then we gorge ourselves.

If we're twenty-eight, we take the five thousand dollars Grandma left us in her will and run down to the store and get this really top-of-the-line sound system for our car, and we toss away the perfectly good system that had been in there.

Being impious goes beyond ignoring the fact that we're in another's debt. It also includes doing some things despite the fact that we know better, despite the fact that we were brought up better than how we're acting right now.

As we learn more about God's love for us, we realize how much he has given us and how much of our devotion he deserves. As we reach adulthood, we realize how much our parents and other elders in our life have done for us and how much of our devotion they deserve.

Our impiety, then, is one of the ways we squander what we've been given. Because of God and others, we have

THE SPIRIT AND THE SACRAMENT OF CONFIRMATION

within us the ability to show devotion, to show proper gratitude. But we take that ability—and the time and effort it demands—and blow it on ourselves, one way or another. We spend those gifts, those advantages, those blessings, on us, us, us.

Impiety wraps us up in ourselves. Piety leads us back to the ones and the One who have given us so much (made us who we are, in every good sense). More than that, it leads us to others. We are able to love God because he loves us. He has shown us love and has demonstrated what love means. We are able to be a good parent, spouse, friend, coworker, or neighbor because as we were growing in wisdom, age, and grace we had a good parent.

So, as a tribute to that parent, we now are called on to be a good person. In a sense, we can't pay back what we have been given. We can only give what we have now. Part of that payment is to those who gave us so much and part is to others.

Piety is: We were given and now we give.

Impiety is: We were given and now we give only to ourselves.

On Piety and Devotion

Piety is the foundation of all the virtues.

—*ST. AMBROSE (CA. 340–397)*

THE SPIRIT AND THE SACRAMENT OF CONFIRMATION

The royal virtues are principally two: justice and piety.

—ST. ISIDORE OF SEVILLE (CA. 560–636)

For it is the nature of love, to love when it feels itself loved, and to love all things loved of its beloved. So when the soul has by degrees known the love of its Creator toward it, it loves him, and loving him, loves all things whatsoever that God loves.

—ST. CATHERINE OF SIENA (CA. 1347–1380)

Do not show signs of devotion outwardly when you have none within.

—ST. TERESA OF ÁVILA (1515–1582)

Charity and devotion differ no more, the one from the other, than the flame from the fire.

—ST. FRANCIS DE SALES (1567–1622)

A Prayer for Piety

Come, Holy Spirit, today through your gift of piety, let my actions be my thanks. Let my life be my adoration of the One who gives me all. Amen.

CHAPTER EIGHT

Charisms and the Charismatic Renewal Movement

The Gift of Fear of the Lord: Does God Still Smiteth People?

We're blessed to live in a time that has seen a "rebirth" of the workings of the Holy Spirit.

Of course, the Spirit has always been a part of creation since the dawn of time, and a part of the church since the time of Jesus and the apostles.

Still, in the future, historians will likely look back on the end of the twentieth century and note how the Spirit rattled the rafters once again, not just within the church on earth as a whole, but also in countries, regions, parishes, and small groups of laity—in the minds and hearts and souls of individuals.

Recent times have been, to put it mildly, interesting. The Holy Spirit saw to it that the second millennium ended with a whoosh, not a whimper.

What was that whoosh? It was an amazing new chapter in the continuing unfolding of the Pentecost story. Who knew? Who even suspected? In early 1959, the benevolent (and frumpy-looking) Pope John XXIII announced his plans to convene an ecumenical council. He had been in office for only ninety days.

According to Papa John, this wasn't something he had cooked up. It was the Holy Spirit's idea.

Ultimately, the result was the Second Vatican Council, at which the church—then, as always, under the guidance of the Spirit—reexamined itself and its role in the world and in the lives of individual people, and redefined itself, not with new truths but with new language, explaining and presenting truths that do not—that cannot—change.

At that time in the Catholic Church—and for a long, long time before that within Christianity as a whole—the dramatic manifestations of the Spirit were seen more as history than as here-and-now occurrences. These manifestations were viewed as limited to a few select saints, not lavishly doled out to what we might call "the general public."

What were those early manifestations? Or, rather, what *are* they?

Formally, they're known as charisms. The Greek word *kharisma* means "divine favor." The same root can be found in *charis*, "grace," and *chara*, "joy."

Kharismata—the plural form of the Greek *kharisma*—aren't things somebody owes us. We haven't earned them.

They are, to use a modern analogy, "unbirthday presents," gifts given out of the blue, "just because."

But they're not really given "just because." They're given because God loves us. Because, as Pope John Paul II wrote in his encyclical, the Spirit is the gift.

———

Jesus told the apostles they would perform signs and miracles. He told them that he was going to leave and the Spirit was going to come. Now we can see, from the writings in the New Testament, that the two are intimately related. The apostles and others in the early church were able to do those things because the Spirit came, because the Spirit stayed.

What *are* these charisms? They are gifts from God that are to be used for the glory of God. They are, for example, as St. Paul lists in 1 Corinthians 12:4–11 and Romans 12:6–8, prophecy, wisdom, knowledge, extraordinary faith, discernment of spirits, healing, working miracles, speaking in tongues, and interpretation of tongues.

But, the apostle warns, these gifts should be things Christians pray for and desire for the good of the community and not simply for their own satisfaction (1 Corinthians 14:1–19).

In our own era, the bishops at Vatican II put it this way in *Lumen Gentium:*

It is not only through the sacraments and the ministries of the church that the Holy Spirit sanctifies and leads the People of God and enriches it with virtues, but "allotting his gifts to everyone according as he wills"(1 Corinthians 12:11), he distributes special graces among the faithful of every rank. By these gifts he makes them fit and ready to undertake the various tasks and offices which contribute toward the renewal and building up of the church, according to the words of the Apostle: "The manifestation of the Spirit is given to everyone for profit" (1 Corinthians 12:7). These charisms, whether they be the more outstanding or the more simple and widely diffused, are to be received with thanksgiving and consolation, for they are perfectly suited to and useful for the needs of the church. Extraordinary gifts are not to be sought after, nor are the fruits of apostolic labor to be presumptuously expected from their use, but judgment as to their genuity and proper use belongs to those who are appointed leaders in the church, to whose special competence it belongs, not indeed to extinguish the Spirit, but to test all things and hold fast to that which is good (cf. 1 Thessalonians 5:12; 19–21). (12)

Lumen Gentium was promulgated—declared—by Pope Paul VI on November 21, 1964. At that time, the "more simple and widely diffused" charisms were commonly accepted as a part of a Catholic's life, but "extraordinary gifts" were, by and large, unheard of. As one Catholic dictionary (published before the council) put it, when it came to those more outstanding charisms, "they were [a] more frequent occurrence in the early church than they are today."

That frequency in the church would increase dramatically within the five years after *Lumen Gentium.*

We'll get to what's seen as a landmark event in the modern movement, but first we need to repeat that from the time of the apostles until the latter half of the twentieth century, the Spirit wasn't asleep at the switch. That's an impossibility. As the *Catechism* says, quoting St. Augustine, "What the soul is to the human body, the Holy Spirit is to the Body of Christ, which is the Church" (section 797).

Within the larger church, within all Christianity, the Spirit was stirring in a particular way in the late nineteenth and early twentieth centuries among a variety of assemblies, sects, and churches that came to be known as Pentecostal. They sprang from the preaching of revivalists, especially among American Baptist and Methodist congregations.

As their name implies, they were marked by charismatic goings-on, particularly speaking in tongues and faith healing.

Within the Catholic Church, a movement began, which came to be called the Catholic Charismatic Renewal. It generally marks its beginning at a 1967 retreat for college students at the Ark and the Dove retreat house outside Pittsburgh,

Pennsylvania. The Spirit was stirring in a particular way at the end of the 1960s. Like the variety of seismic activities before a volcano blows, there were rumblings in several areas.

Throughout that particular weekend, the young people had been praying for a "New Pentecost." On Saturday evening, a handful were in the chapel when it came. When that group failed to go to the dining room for a birthday party, others went to find out what had delayed them. They likewise were filled with the Spirit.

The "charismatic renewal" within the Catholic Church took off and spread quickly. Those who were "baptized in the Spirit" frequently received special gifts from him, charisms that echoed those written about in Acts and in the works of St. Paul.

Many individuals experienced a deepening and personalizing of their relationship with Jesus. The Scriptures "came alive." Speaking in tongues—the gift of glossolalia (we'll get to that in a moment)—was part of many small prayer groups.

It's important to point out that this wasn't the creation of a new church. Rather, it was the Spirit at work within the church created by Christ. Still, as the bishops had written during Vatican II, it was up to authorities in the church "not . . . to extinguish the Spirit, but to test all things and hold fast to that which is good."

In 1976, the American bishops offered their cautious support to what was taking place within and through what had become a movement. Historians say they hesitated because of past problems concerning some Protestant charismatics who deny the authority of the bishops and the worth of the seven sacraments and who promote biblical fundamentalism.

In time, both Pope Paul VI and Pope John Paul II offered their support to the charismatic renewal within the Catholic Church. By the end of the twentieth century, the renewal was characterized by a strong biblically based devotion to the Eucharist and to Mary and by its solid backing of the pontiff.

By then, too, the Holy Spirit was using the movement to renew and enliven in new ways, not just individuals, but also communities, parishes, schools, dioceses, countries, and the church worldwide. "Charismatics" became part of mainstream Catholicism at every level.

Another distinguishing feature of the movement remains the high percentage of laity involved. That fact was emphasized at a time when, in western Europe and North America, vocations to the priesthood and to religious life declined sharply.

As John Paul II noted in a general audience in the mid-1990s: "We cannot but admire the great wealth of gifts bestowed by the Holy Spirit on lay people as members of the church in our age, as well [as in the early church.] Each of them has the necessary ability to carry out the tasks to which he is called for the welfare of the Christian people, and the work of salvation, if he is open, docile, and faithful to the Holy Spirit's action."

The Holy Father reminded his listeners that "the primary or principal aim of many charisms is not the personal sanctification of those who receive them, but the service of others and the welfare of the church . . . in that it concerns the growth of Christ's Mystical Body."

———≈———

Theologians explain that charismatic gifts are called *gratiae gratis datae,* or "graces gratuitously given." And as such, they differ from *gratia gratum faciens,* grace given for the sanctification of the person who receives it. Both—in all forms—are from God.

What are those charisms, specifically? A list generally includes the following:

- Faith. Not the theological virtue—of the trio faith, hope, and love—but a faith that can work miracles. Prominent theologians have defined it as bravely and consistently confessing, preaching, and defending the faith, especially in times of persecution. It can also be explained as profound certitude about the truths of the faith and the ability to teach them clearly.

- Power to express knowledge. This, also, is the ability to teach or preach sacred truth with exactness and clarity. While the Holy Spirit's gift of knowledge is for the benefit of the one receiving the gift, the power to express knowledge is for teaching others. The fathers and doctors of the church had this charism.

- Wisdom in discourse. Again, though the same word is used, this isn't the gift we looked at in chapter 2. (Although, of course, it *is* a gift of the Holy Spirit.) Since this has to do with serving others, it's demonstrated by preaching or teaching sacred doctrine and by giving spiritual direction. But unlike the power to express knowledge, this gift allows its recipient to also truly feel and experience the truth.

- Gift of tongues. This is probably the most often cited of the charismatic gifts. It takes a couple of different forms. "Glossolalia" usually refers to what we might call an incoherent babbling that's not understood by the speaker or the listener. And cases of glossolalia can be the result of mental or physical problems or even have diabolical roots.

  However, when it's a charism sent by the Spirit it's a form of prayer. It may include moans, cries, or what sounds like words.

  The name also refers to what happened on Pentecost: the sudden and inexplicable ability to speak a foreign language.

- Interpretation of tongues. This gift allows a person to understand an unintelligible language—to hear someone speaking in tongues—and to translate it for others.

- Prophecy. St. Paul put it this way: "Those who speak in a tongue do not speak to other people but to God; for nobody understands them, since they are speaking mysteries in the Spirit. On the other hand, those who prophesy speak to other people for their upbuilding and encouragement and consolation" (1 Corinthians 14:2–3).

  Both prophecy—which shouldn't be confused with fortunetelling—and revelations (insights) have to do with announcing and proclaiming divine truths for the building up of the community.

- Discernment of spirits. This gift gives one the ability to name the cause of certain phenomena or the spirit from which they occur. The ability itself can be increased through study and experience, but this term means the God-given gift. It's important because a number of phenomena (as we said with glossolalia) can have a variety of possible sources: natural, supernatural, or diabolical.

- Healing and miraculous powers. Along with speaking in tongues, healing is the gift probably most often associated with the charismatic renewal. Miracles do happen. That's not to say that all healings facilitated by this gift are miraculous. Sometimes the cure is what we might call "natural," although, of course, the ultimate source is always God. The person who has this charism, acting as an instrument of God, may have the ability to do what those with human power alone cannot.

While the charisms of the "New Pentecost" have infused the church, the Charismatic Renewal Movement is still also an organization. Typically, its members are the ones sponsoring a prayer group at the parish level. And it's at such a group that one would be able to get more information about the movement.

The Gift of Fear of the Lord: Does God Still Smiteth People?

We humans love circles. The best story starts here, goes around and around and around, and ends up not there but—surprise!—here again.

That describes our lives. Created by God, we spend our days returning to him. We do that whether we realize it or not. Our God, that supremely generous supreme being, doesn't insist we return to him. He doesn't force us to spend eternity with him. We can choose to go elsewhere. We can choose hell.

Then the circle is lost. The circle is broken. Coming from God, created by God, saved by God, we can be with God or be without him.

With the seventh gift of the Holy Spirit, we wrap back around to the first. Fear of the Lord leads to wisdom. More than that, it's the beginning of wisdom. This is stated in a number of passages from Scripture, including Job 28:28; Psalm 115:11; Proverbs 1:7; and Sirach 1:14. We'll look at those in a moment.

As with the other six gifts, this one must be important and valuable even if we, in our own time, don't quite understand why that's so or how that's so. Still, as mentioned in chapter 1, Isaiah used it when he prophesied about the coming Messiah. He wrote that the Christ, the Anointed One, was going to possess and demonstrate fear of the Lord.

And if we are to imitate Christ, which of course we are, then . . . what? We're supposed to think of this loving Father, this "Abba," this Daddy, and tremble in our boots?

Do we need fortitude just to approach God because we can't do it without being afraid? What kind of an all-loving God is that?

Believers today seem to have all kinds of problems with this fear-of-the-Lord business. It appears to be a throwback to an era when children were considered a father's property or, at best, were to be seen but not heard.

It doesn't seem likely that a gift of the Holy Spirit would have grown to be outdated or that it would have served its earthly purpose and now its time has passed. Still, there's something about this gift that doesn't seem like a gift to us now. At first glance, it appears to be more of a—well, as long as we're looking at it through a contemporary lens—dysfunction.

We're one big happy family, but we're afraid of Dad. More than that: We're *supposed to be* afraid of Dad. And even more than that: Dad considers our being afraid of him a *gift* to us.

It's tempting to think that any explanation of this supposed gift is going to sound as hollow as some poor mom's positive spin on a dad's senseless if not cruel comment: "Honey, when your father says ____, you know what he really means is ____. He just has a hard time finding the right words. . . . He's always had trouble expressing himself when it comes to . . ."

Except this isn't a human parent, one who's meanspirited or well-intentioned but inept at communicating. This is *God*. When we speak of his Spirit, we generally put the word *Holy* in front of it, and very rightly so. He knows everything. He can certainly find the right words.

So this gift is good. It's great, and the words fit well. Writers of the Old Testament use these words many times, and these writers were, the church points out, inspired by the Holy Spirit.

Each gift is not just a word but a concept revealed to us humans. In them, God is saying generously, "Look, I'll get more specific about you and me." That concept, that idea, which the words are supposed to convey, remains firm and valuable. But the words themselves—or, rather, that one specific word—can in our own time cause us to stumble a bit.

This gift combines fear and our relationship to God. How do we put them together and why should we? A good place to begin that examination is those four Old Testament references.

It's Job who declares, "And he [God] said to humankind, / 'Truly, the fear of the Lord, that is wisdom; / and to depart from evil is understanding'" (Job 28:28).

Psalm 115:11 tells us, "You who fear the Lord, trust in the Lord! / He is their help and their shield."

Proverbs 1:7 reads, "The fear of the Lord is the beginning of knowledge; / fools despise wisdom and instruction."

And Sirach 1:14 says, "To fear the Lord is the beginning of wisdom; / she is created with the faithful in the womb."

What do they mean? Scripture scholars point out that the entire twenty-eighth chapter of Job focuses on where wisdom is found and that the final verse is considered a later addition. One way or another, it adds a twist to the poem. (Just as the final gift adds a twist to the list.) The first twenty-seven verses say wisdom is inaccessible, and the last one tells people that the only way for them to reach it is through "fear of the Lord." And here, that phrase means piety and service.

Ah, piety. We've examined that (in chapter 7). And service to . . . ? God, of course. But we can look at the idea of service through a Gospel perspective. That tells us that whatever we do to the least among us, we do to Christ himself (see Matthew 25:31–46). By serving them, we are serving God.

Scripture scholars also say that it seems to them that Psalm 115, which is only eighteen verses, is made up of three sections: the beginning of a communal lament, some hymn-like passages, and a call to trust in God's blessing and the assurance of it. Israel is to trust in the Lord. The house of Aaron is to trust in the Lord. And those who fear the Lord are to trust in the Lord. For members of each category, the Lord "is their help and their shield."

Those scholars say that the quote from Proverbs states the entire theme of that book. "Fear of the Lord" is a recurring phrase that refers to a reverential and loving obedience to the will of God. Proverbs also continues to point out the contrast between wisdom and foolishness.

And scholars note that Sirach begins with the author telling readers that he has investigated life, wisdom, and foolishness and now is reporting his findings. After a brief prologue, the author launches into a praise of wisdom and then examines its relationship to this seventh gift of the Spirit.

- It is glory and exultation.
- It is gladness and a crown of rejoicing.
- It delights the heart and gives joy and long life.
- Those who practice it will have a happy end, and on the day of their death they will be blessed.
- It is fullness of wisdom.
- It is the crown of wisdom, making peace and perfect health flourish.
- It is the root of wisdom, and "her branches are long life."
- It is wisdom and discipline, and "fidelity and humility are his delight."

CHARISMS AND THE CHARISMATIC RENEWAL MOVEMENT

The author warns his readers that they aren't to "disobey the fear of the Lord." They aren't to approach God "with a divided mind." If we are hypocrites and "exalt" ourselves and bring dishonor upon ourselves, we're in big trouble. The Lord is going to reveal our secrets, the author tells us, and is going to overthrow us before the whole congregation because we "did not come in the fear of the Lord" and our hearts were "full of deceit."

Sirach's second chapter continues with our duties toward God. We're going to be tested like gold in a fire, he says. If we fear the Lord, we wait for his mercy and we don't stray. We trust in him and our reward isn't lost. We hope for good things, for lasting joy and mercy.

The author asks if anyone has persevered in the fear of the Lord and been forsaken. Again, we need to consider how we need the gift of fortitude, which doesn't eliminate hard times and suffering. But sticking with the Lord is the best choice because he is compassionate and merciful. And—a big plus for all of us—he forgives sins.

It's those with "timid hearts" and "slack hands" who are in serious trouble, as are those sinners who walk "a double path." He doesn't say sinners, period; if that were the case, we'd all be in for it. No, it's the ones who are faint-hearted and have no trust in God, the ones who have lost their nerve; they are the ones who won't receive any "shelter."

On the other hand, if we *do* fear the Lord, we:

- do not disobey his words but, rather, love him and keep his ways
- seek to please him and to love him and are filled with his law
- prepare our hearts and humble ourselves before him

One more point before we leave Sirach. After he concludes his second chapter by telling us to "fall into the hands of the Lord, but not into the hands of mortals," he launches into chapter 3 with the duties of a child toward his or her parents: duty to God, first; duty to parents, next—the very definition of piety.

Haveing fear of the Lord is living the law. It's living the commandments, especially those first four, as mentioned in the chapter on piety: the first three dealing with our relationship with God, the next one with our relationship with our parents.

We don't love our parents because we are afraid of them. We don't love God because he makes us tremble with fright. Even though "fear of the Lord" can be found throughout an English-language Bible, it's a phrase that doesn't really match the different Hebrew and Greek terms from which it is translated.

What the original words mean is experiencing and knowing God as completely holy, completely "other," absolute, all-powerful, all-knowing. If we have this gift, we

CHARISMS AND THE CHARISMATIC RENEWAL MOVEMENT

detest our sins because we see how offensive they are when compared to God's love for us.

As we gain this gift, we begin to see more clearly that what we have done is horrible. But we don't fear punishment or even damnation. No, we simply see that God deserves better from us.

We can't *really* "let God down" in the sense that we disappoint him. That's a very human expression for a very human emotion. And, needless to say, we can't really influence an all-powerful being that way. Why not? Because if we can really make God happy or sad, then we have some control over God and he would have some limits. But we don't, and he doesn't.

Rather, we use those terms, those idioms, because they're so familiar to us. Our feeble minds don't understand the reality. That's okay. We don't have to be able to verbalize it to live it. And having fear of the Lord is living in a way that pleases the Lord—but more accurately, it's living in the way in which he created us to live.

And again—to beat the drum one more time—he gives us a choice and lets us decide. If we fear the Lord, then we can more deeply experience his love and more readily recognize the relationship between our loving of him and our serving of others. We want to praise him, worship him, adore him. We want to live the life he created us for because he knows best and because we—almost selfishly—recognize that's the best life for us, the one that will bring us the greatest joy and the one that leads to everlasting joy.

So fear of the Lord has to do with learning more about God, which could be through worship, through personal prayer, through study, and through action. We meet Christ face to face in a unique way when we come face to face with "the least" among us.

Fear of the Lord nudges us in that direction. And, truth be told, when we begin to look at our lives and our decisions in that light, it can be scary. God isn't frightening, but what he suggests can be terrifying.

We aren't alone in feeling that way. Time and again in Scripture, when someone was asked to do something by a supernatural visitor (a vision from Yahweh, an angel popping in), the person being visited was scared. And the first words out of the visitor's mouth were, "Don't be afraid. It's okay. It's all going to be okay."

Most of us won't have visions. Most of us won't see angels. But still we experience that "call." We—through fear of the Lord—realize what our mission is. Or, more accurately, we experience that series of calls, that series of missions. Most likely we can't see how each will unfold; we can only realize how we are to begin.

Often at first glance, and even at second, what God proposes to us personally appears to make little sense. "Who, *me?* You want *me* to . . . ?" Fear of the Lord helps us realize that the seemingly impossible can happen not because of us but because of the all-powerful God who so deeply loves us.

Fear of the Lord helps us understand "I'm only his instrument. He chose me not because I'm who I am but because he's who he is. Any credit rightly goes to him first and foremost."

We get some kudos, too, of course, because God invites and doesn't demand. He lets us say yes or no. So we aren't like a flute that a musician picks up and plays. There really is no good comparison because there really is nothing like the relationship we have with God or the closer relationship with him he's always ready to offer us.

Again, we decide.

Just as the early church, "living in the fear of the Lord and in the comfort of the Holy Spirit, . . . increased in numbers" (Acts 9:31), we can increase in the Spirit's amazing grace by doing the same.

Very near the end of the New Testament, in 1 John, is a passage on fear of the Lord that says it all: "There is no fear in love, but perfect loves casts out fear; for fear has to do with punishment, and whoever fears has not reached perfection in love" (1 John 4:18).

So as we grow in the gift, we begin to fear God's punishment less even as we begin to fear offending him more. We fear not loving him as we should or not serving others as we should. Again (and again and again) the two duties cannot be separated, not in the early church and not now.

"We love because he first loved us," John writes. "Those who say 'I love God,' and hate their brothers or sisters, are liars; for those who do not love a brother or sister whom they have seen, cannot love God whom they have not seen. The commandment we have from him is this: those who love God must love their brothers and sisters also" (1 John 4:19–21).

Just a few verses before those, John gives the same message and includes the role of the third person of the Blessed Trinity. Love is from God. God revealed his love by sending his Son so that we can live through him. Since God loves us so much, we ought to love one another. If we love one another, God lives in us and his love is perfected in us.

"By this we know that we abide in him and he in us, because he has given us of his Spirit" (1 John 4:13).

Fear of the Lord is the realization of God's incredible love for us, which helps us also come to realize how much we should love him and others. Fear of the Lord—then, now, and always—comes from the Spirit.

On the Flip Side: You're Not the Boss of Me!

It's possible to practice the opposite of fear of the Lord in a couple of different ways. Each has to do with how we control God—or, at least, how we believe we do that.

We can declare—by word and deed—that God is the absentee landlord of the universe. Yes, he got the ball rolling, but then he . . . Well, we don't know exactly where he went or what he's doing now, but he's not around. He plays no role in the unfolding of creation or in our life. This isn't really a lack

187

of faith. We still believe that, yes, there is a God. It's more putting a condition on who, or what, God is: Yes, there is a God, but . . .

A second way we can try to control God in our lives is by trying to stuff the creator into a cubbyhole—one that, we believe, makes our life much easier. This is the Sunday-only God. The holy-cow-I'm-in-deep-trouble-and-need-a-miracle-from-you-*now* God. We give him more room to roam than if he were that absentee landlord, but he still has his place, and it's where we choose to place him.

In this approach, "religion" (go to Mass on Sunday, don't kill anybody) does not mix with "life" (everything that is not religion). We may be fulfilling our duties to the letter, but the words themselves are lifeless. They have no . . . Spirit.

If we had to come up with a name for this need to control God—this fault, this sin—idolatry might be a good one. We don't form a golden calf and worship it. Rather, we look in the mirror and declare, "Oooh, baby, you're the boss."

It's not as though God is the queen bee and we're all drones. It *could* be that way, except God loves us. We're not mindless automatons. But we're not gods. We're not God. We can't control God, and if we choose to ignore God it doesn't mean God is no longer God.

But how do we find him—hear him—in our own lives here and now? First, we need to listen. After all, how do we hear anything? We have to be quieter than the sound we're attempting to hear. And sometimes God whispers. He isn't in the strong wind, earthquake, or fire but in the small breeze (see 1 Kings 19:11–13).

We must pay attention to his advice: "Be still, and know that I am God!" (Psalm 46:10). "Be still" is a polite way of saying, "Shut up for a minute, will ya?"

The opposite of fear of the Lord seems disrespectful and foolish if we begin to listen to God. God isn't absent. He's present, omnipresent—everywhere, all the time. He can't be pigeonholed, and his love helps us avoid doing the same things to ourselves and others.

If we listen to the voice and do what he asks, we'll be surprised. Amazed. Blessed. We'll be like the waiters at the wedding feast in Cana (John 2:1–12). "Do whatever he tells you," Mary said to them. Uh-huh. And that was . . . fill those big old jars with water, draw some out, and let your boss sample it. That certainly made no sense. And weren't those servants going to look like idiots when the headwaiter asked, "Just what do you think you're doing? This is water!"

Small wonder people sometimes fear God in the commonly understood definition of the word *fear*. First, he actually does speak to folks—even today. He speaks to us through Scripture, sometimes in our hearts, sometimes through a messenger—a friend, a stranger, an event, a word. Through, always in one way or another, the Spirit.

CHARISMS AND THE CHARISMATIC RENEWAL MOVEMENT

God speaks to each of us. Why wouldn't he? He loves each of us no less than anyone else he ever created or ever will create. Name a biblical bigwig or a saint. God loves you as much as he loves him or her. God wants the same for you that he wanted for that person. God himself wants this. He wants each of us to have the best. Forever.

But the thought of hearing his voice can be scary. And, often, it's more frightening still to consider actually doing what he recommends. It's good that he quickly adds, "Don't be afraid." How can we not be?

John told us how. The more we love, the less afraid we are of God's will for us. That makes sense. The more we love, the more we come to know, the more we come to trust.

So the opposite then of fear of the Lord also includes a lack of trust in God based on a lack of love of God. That goes back to a lack of knowledge of God—not a theology-degree knowledge but a "sit down, shut up, and listen" knowledge.

Or, more accurately, it's a "sit down, shut up, listen, and then speak" knowledge. Conversation is the very definition of *prayer*. And any good conversationalist knows that it isn't the speaking that helps you make a connection but listening and being open to the other person.

We must listen for, look for, and be open to what God has to say to us personally.

On Fear of the Lord

Let us fear the Lord Jesus, whose blood was given for us; let us respect our leaders; let us honor the presbyters; let us teach the young in the school of the fear of God.

—POPE CLEMENT I (D. CA. 97)

Fear the Lord, then, and you will do everything well.

—HERMAS (FIRST OR SECOND CENTURY)

For I have learned for a fact that nothing so effectively obtains, retains and regains grace, as that we should always be found not high-minded before God, but filled with holy fear.

—ST. BERNARD OF CLAIRVAUX (1090–1153)

Fear God, and you shall have no need of being afraid of man.

—THOMAS À KEMPIS (CA. 1379–1471)

We must fear God through love, not love him through fear.

—BISHOP JEAN-PIERRE CAMUS DE PONT-CARRÉ (1584–1652)

A Prayer for Fear of the Lord

Come, Holy Spirit, today help me accept the gift of the fear of the Lord, the offer to love you more deeply, more fully, more selflessly. You who are the love of God, you who deserve my all. Amen.

CHAPTER NINE

Now What?

*Developing Your
Personal Relationship
with the Holy Spirit*

Assuming these seven gifts and the multitude of graces that accompany them are good things, how do we get them? How do we get even one?

The wonderful part about God's love is not just that it's freely given but that it further frees the one to whom it is given. We need only ask. Then we need only then use what we are given.

Use how? One way or another, to better accept Jesus, to better share with others the Good News about him.

Spread the Good News? In our own time and in our own country that idea can seem a little silly. After all, the vast majority of the population has heard the name and knows about him, sort of. However, even those who have religiously practiced the Christian religion all their lives may not really know the Good News, in the sense of experiencing the profound joy it can bring and the profound peace that comes from meeting Christ on a more personal level.

Many of us tend to be like the pre-Pentecost apostles: filled with belief but timid, loving the Lord deeply but keeping ourselves tucked away in an upper room.

It's the Spirit who sets hearts and minds on fire, helping us better recognize just who Jesus is and what he did—and what he does.

In our own time and country, we don't fear martyrdom. Yes, there are those who die for the faith, but it's typically not in places that allow religious freedom. No, what we fear is becoming, well, a "Jesus freak."

If we *really* allow the Spirit in, is he going to make us look like—or really be—an idiot? Don't give that concern a second thought. The answer is yes and no: we may well look like one, but we aren't being one.

Yes, we may look like an idiot, because the father of lies—Satan—is alive and kicking in our own time. In many ways he dominates much of the world and his opinion is accepted as gospel.

But what he says isn't true. And that's why the answer is also no, we will not actually be an idiot if we allow the Spirit in. We will be—through God's blessing—what St. Paul refers to as "fools for Christ" (see 1 Corinthians 4:10). Not a true fool—we talked about those in chapter 2—but one who seems to be foolish in the eyes of those who don't know, accept, or live what is true.

What is true? Jesus. He is truth (John 14:6).

And Truth will always, ultimately, defeat Deceit because Truth already has. To use an analogy, the game continues but the outcome is already known. We simply choose which side we wish to be on. Fortunately, when we find ourselves on the wrong team—the one that, to many folks' way of thinking, seems to be winning—we can switch sides, thanks to God's mercy and forgiveness.

But let's get back to the seven gifts and how to get them. One of the great things about them is that the Spirit will give us exactly what we need, sometimes just when we need it. At *that* moment there is a providential nudge, or the words are there for us, or the right choice becomes clear. (He is the great Counselor.) Sometimes the nudge—the words, the choice—comes long before we need it.

He may prepare us. He may anticipate what we will need or perhaps what another will need from us. (Although, as mentioned in chapter 4, we may never be called on to use what we have been given.)

Still, is it really as simple as asking and then using? Yes. Is it always easy? No.

The asking isn't tough. We just can't be shy. Don't tap on that door; beat on it (see Matthew 7:7).

But the using is a different story . . . It may well be that what the Holy Spirit has in mind for us, what he invites us to do, is something we would rather avoid. We want to RSVP,

"Sorry. Busy." (As St. Augustine wrote: Make me chaste, Lord, but not yet.)

But, of course, the more we use a gift, the more of that gift we receive and the better we become at recognizing that gift in our life.

Because we were made in God's image, some of the things we do reflect God. We can see him in us. That's true with gifts. Imagine being a parent with two adult children. We present each with a brand-new car. One uses his all the time. He drives it here, there, and everywhere; gets into a fender-bender now and then; and quickly racks ups more than one hundred thousand miles. The other child put his car in the garage and hasn't moved it.

Now who gets a new car, or, rather, which child gets an even newer car?

Yes, as a parent we would want to try to keep the giving relatively even, but the point here is this: if you don't drive the car, you don't need a newer one or a better one. If you drive it until the wheels are ready to fall off, you do.

The Spirit wants us to use his gifts until the wheels fall off.

He wants to give us the "new and improved" wisdom, understanding, counsel, and so on.

Except, as we know, the gifts can't really be new and improved. Only our ability to accept them and use them can be. We can accept them more. We can use them more.

It's easier to do that if we come to know the Spirit more, if our relationship deepens—which, when one thinks about it, is truly amazing. God, the creator and sustainer of all—the one who is, was, and always will be—wants to have a personal relationship with each of us. With you.

Because we're human—body and soul—the third person of this Being is already in us; as St. Augustine said, he is closer to us than we are to ourselves. The Lord and Giver of Life wants to have a personal relationship with each of us. With you.

How do we further it? How do we deepen it?

Again, consider how we creatures are like our Creator. Look at how we do things well among ourselves, and then apply that to the relationship between a single human and God.

We can't be friends with someone if we don't know her. We get to know her by spending time with her, by telling her about ourselves, by listening to her speak of herself. Over time, that person plays a more important role in our life. Over time, friendship deepens into love.

It's the same deal with God, mostly. The difference is that the Spirit already loves us completely, with his infinite love. Nothing we have done, nothing we do, nothing we could ever do or will ever do will stop that love or even lessen that love.

That love will never betray us, never want anything but the best for us, never offer us anything but the best.

But while the Spirit knows us and loves us, it's up to us to come to better know and love him. Part of that depends on prayer—the time spent talking and listening. (And since this is God, adoring and praising are part of it, too. Piety, remember?) And part of it depends on finding out more about the Spirit, through the reading of Scripture (hey, he wrote the Book, after all), through study and research (That can sound grim, but it simply means reading what others have written about the Spirit, especially what the saints have said. Then, too, it could be going to a talk on the Spirit or being brave enough to drop in on the parish's charismatic prayer meeting.), through service to others (We have to use those gifts! We have to rack up those miles on our "car."), and through the sacraments, especially reconciliation and the Eucharist.

In other words, we have to go to confession and go to Mass.

Confession? That can be a tough one, but it's one we need. By our sinning, we can mess up our soul—our very self, where the Holy Spirit is—and if we want to be more open to his promptings, we need to make sure we aren't building barriers. That's what sin is.

The sacrament of reconciliation tears these barriers down. "Repent" was not an infrequent command in Scripture. Jesus certainly was "prorepentance," and so were the apostles. Remember—one more time—Peter's Pentecost address to the crowd.

The rabble: "What do we do?"

Peter: "Repent, and be baptized every one of you in the name of Jesus Christ so that your sins may be forgiven; and you will receive the gift of the Holy Spirit. For the promise is for you, for your children, and for all who are far away, everyone whom the Lord our God calls to him" (Acts 2:38–39).

("All who are far away" includes us. We are "far away" from that place and year in distance and time.)

But we have to stop thinking the word *repent* implies that we're the scum of the earth. We're not. God made us much better than that. Repenting means admitting we've misused what God has given us, being sorry about those choices, and making a promise not to continue them.

Then what? Then, just as on the first Pentecost, the Spirit flows in.

In addition to getting to know the Spirit through the sacrament of reconciliation, we get to better know him at Mass, where he and we are with the resurrected Christ in a particular way, a way Christ set up for us. Christ did all that during his earthly life because he was filled with the Spirit, and it was the same Christ who breathed on his apostles on Easter Sunday night and gave them the Spirit (see John 20:22).

The truth is, the reality is, the truly Good News is that any day—every day—can be Pentecost.

The truth is, the reality is, the truly Good News is that today can be Pentecost for you.

Come Today, Holy Spirit

Come, Holy Spirit, today help me pause. Help me consider. Help me ask for, seek out, and recognize wisdom. As you will, help me be your instrument of wisdom for others who are searching, for others who are hurting.

Come, Holy Spirit, today allow me to understand more. I want to see as you see, not just others but myself. You live and move and work in each of us. Help me see you.

Come, Holy Spirit, today lead me to those with wisdom and understanding. Let me be your voice, your touch, your kindness, your blessing to those who seek your counsel. Prepare me to do your will.

Come, Holy Spirit, today guide me in the way of knowledge. Help me learn what I am to learn, help me teach what I am to teach. Always help me come to better know and teach Christ.

Come, Holy Spirit, today give me the courage to make it through my day. Bless me with fortitude to face the hardest challenges of my life. Help me keep my eyes on Easter.

Come, Holy Spirit, today through your gift of piety, let my actions be my thanks. Let my life be my adoration of the One who gives me all.

Come, Holy Spirit, today help me accept the gift of the fear of the Lord, the offer to love you more deeply, more fully, more selflessly. You who are the love of God, you who deserve my all.

Come today, Holy Spirit, come today. Amen.